THE HYMNS OF
WESLEY A[ND]

FIVE INFORM[AL]

CW00547016

BY

BERNARD L. MANNING, M.A.

(Fellow of Jesus College, Cambridge)

THE EPWORTH PRESS

Publisher's Note

Although the commemoration of the 250th anniversary of
the conversions of the Wesley brothers is now past, that
event disclosed a continuing appetite for literature concerned
with the origins and development of Methodism. Not the
least of the interests involved in hymnology and in that field
The Hymns of Wesley and Watts has established itself as a
classic. In the judgment of the Editorial Committee of the
Epworth Press it would be a culpable omission if this book
were not made available to another generation of those
devoted to hymns. It is reproduced entirely in its 1942 form.

John Stacey
Chairman, Editorial Committee,
Epworth Press

Cataloguing in Publication Data available

0 7162 0455 X

First published 1942
Reissued 1988 by
Epworth Press
Room 195 1 Central Buildings
Westminster London SW1H 9NR

Printed in Great Britain by
Richard Clay Ltd, Bungay, Suffolk

CONTENTS

ACKNOWLEDGEMENTS

THE Executors of the late Bernard L. Manning are indebted to the Editor, Dr. Albert Peel, M.A., and the proprietors of the *Congregational Quarterly* for permission to use 'The Hymns of Dr. Isaac Watts'; and to the proprietors of the *Transactions of the Congregational Historical Society* for permission to use 'Some Hymns and Hymn-books'.

FOREWORD

By the REV. HENRY BETT, M.A., LITT.D.

IT must be more than a dozen years ago that I met with a small pamphlet entitled *Christian Experience throughout the Centuries*. It was the report of an address delivered before the Assembly of the Congregational Union, I believe, and the title-page bore the name of Bernard L. Manning, M.A., Fellow and Bursar of Jesus College, Cambridge. I had never heard of Mr. Manning before, but the booklet was of such an extraordinary excellence that I began to look out for anything else that he had written. The next discovery came in 1933, when the *London Quarterly and Holborn Review* published an article under the title 'Hymns for the Use of the People called Methodists'. This was a paper which had been read to the University Methodist Society at Cambridge a few months before. (It is the first essay in this volume.) Now the early part of it was specially interesting to me, not only as a native of Lincolnshire, but because it gave some details of Mr. Manning's early life. I remembered that when I lived in Lincoln between 1911 and 1914, one of the Congregational ministers of the city was the Rev. George Manning. Evidently the writer was his son. I continued to read everything that Mr. Manning wrote, and in *The Spirit of Methodism* I paid him a sincere tribute of admiration. I am very glad now that I did, and I am also glad that I saw him once, when I was on a visit to Cambridge, and my friend the Rev. W. F. Flemington was good enough to invite Mr. Manning to lunch, so that we could meet. As one would expect, he was the most modest of men. Any one might have thought on that occasion that it was he, and not I, who was having the privilege of meeting a man of genius. I went on reading, and recommending to my friends, everything that bore Mr. Manning's name—his two books, *Why not Abandon the Church?* and *Essays in Orthodox Dissent*, and his various articles and addresses. Then a few months ago came the sad news of his untimely death—in my deliberate judgement, the most serious loss that religion in this country has suffered for years past.

Bernard Manning was a religious genius, and one of a

very uncommon type. He was a unique combination—a scholar, a wit, a writer with a remarkably effective English style, and an Evangelical believer. It is not often that you find any one who is all these things at once. His scholarship was never obtruded, but it was always behind all that he wrote. His pleasantly acid wit was a perpetual joy: no one ever poked fun more delightfully at the follies and pretensions of unbelief and at the timidities of conventional religion. But, deeper than all this, there was beneath all that he ever wrote the soul-stirring passion of the Evangelical faith and the Evangelical experience.

Methodism owes a special debt of gratitude to Bernard Manning. I have tried, for forty years past, to recall Methodists to a sense of the greatness of their spiritual heritage in the hymns of the Wesleys. In these hymns we possess a unique treasury of devotional poetry, but we have been neglecting this, and singing instead the flabby and sentimental verses of modern poetasters. It was Bernard Manning, a devoted member of another communion, who told us again of the supreme excellence of our Methodist hymns, and said that the *Collection* of 1780 'ranks with the Psalms, the Book of Common Prayer, the Canon of the Mass. In its own way it is perfect, unapproachable, elemental in its perfection . . . a work of supreme art by a religious genius'.

It is pathetic to remember that the last printed words from Bernard Manning's pen are a sermon preached in Cheshunt College Chapel not very long before he died—a sermon on *The Burial of the Dead*, afterward printed in the *Congregational Quarterly*. At the end of it he quotes some triumphant lines of Charles Wesley's, and nothing could be more appropriate as our farewell to this very gifted man, who was a humble and penitent believer:

> No, dear companion, no:
> We gladly let thee go,
> From a suffering church beneath,
> To a reigning church above:
> Thou hast more than conquer'd death;
> Thou art crown'd with life and love!

HYMNS FOR THE USE OF THE PEOPLE
CALLED METHODISTS[1]

COME with me to John Wesley's own country: Lincoln-shire. Come to the North Wolds, where from the Earl of Yarborough's woods at Pelham's Pillar you can see the line of the Humber and the North Sea, and the Dock Tower of Grimsby by day; and by night the lantern of Spurn lighthouse, the dull glow of Hull on the north, the duller glow of Gains-borough on the west, and between them the flaring furnaces of Scunthorpe. Come to the place where the hill-country of the Wolds ends suddenly with a sharp escarpment. Away to the west stretches the chess-board of variegated woodland, meadows, and ploughed fields till it rises suddenly on a far horizon to that sharp ridge on which, thirty miles away, stands the cathedral church of Lincoln. Half-way down this steep western escarp-ment of the Wolds in the hungry forties of last century, in the ancient Roman town of Caistor, the Methodists built a new chapel, square and high and red, in a county of red bricks and curly red tiles. Inside, the chapel had a deep gallery, and a lofty rostrum. Under the rostrum was the vestry, and through a trap door in the rostrum floor the preacher climbed from the vestry to his place. You saw him enter the vestry below by an ordinary door, and then in due time appeared his head and beard, and you hoped he would forget to shut the trap door, but he never did.

In that chapel it was my fortune to hear many sermons and to be bored by not a few. I am not less grateful for those that bored me than for those which held me interested; for in the effort to escape from boredom I made the most of the resources of my grandfather's pew. Attempts to read the one plain tablet at the side of the rostrum always failed. I grew weary of won-dering why the bright yellow blinds were fitted only on the

[1] A paper read to the University Methodist Society at Wesley Church, Cambridge, on Sunday, November 20, 1932.

south side of the chapel, not on the north (I was very young, you see). I knew by heart the beauties of the thin iron pillars painted by some very ingenious person to deceive us into thinking they were marble. I had to wait for the hymns before the boy who blew the organ would begin his attractive diving and jumping. I had tried to imagine what would really happen if I suddenly put both my hands on the bald head of our friend there in the pew in front until the fascination of the experiment became so great that I was compelled for safety's sake to put away the thought. What, then, was left? Only the pile of Bibles and hymn-books in the left-hand corner. The Bibles, I regret to confess, did not attract me; but *Wesley's Hymns*, *Wesley's Hymns with a Supplement*, and *Wesley's Hymns with New Supplement*, upon these I fell week after week. And there in that pew began an unregulated, passionate, random reading which has gone on ever since.

I could inflict upon you, but I will not, a description of the other chapel that I knew well in those days: the 1662 meeting house of my father's Congregational Church. There I found sermons less dull, for my father preached them; but the casual ministrations of strangers drove me to Part II of Dr. Barrett's *Hymnal*, where among 'Ancient Hymns of the Church' I found Irons's noble translation of the most moving of all medieval hymns—*Dies Irae;* and from *Dies Irae,* not knowing what I did, I caught the infection of a love of Medieval Christianity. To boring sermons, then, I owe two of the best things that I know.

Now, few of you have Methodist grandfathers at Caistor; few of you hear boring Methodist sermons; and, even if you did, few of you would still find your old hymn-books left in the pew. I may be wrong, but I suspect that many of you hardly know even the outward and visible signs of the hymn-book about which I am to talk; and I propose, therefore, before we try to approach its inward and spiritual grace to discuss its external make-up. The power of the late Wesleyan Conference was so great that when in 1904 it said 'Let there be a new hymn-book', behold, it was so. Old hymn-books passed away; all hymn-books became new. Henceforth you were to know only your new hymn-book of 1904, which came in when I was only a boy, but which still left the old on the pew shelves for my research.

I do not speak of it, *The Methodist Hymn-Book*, with its commonplace title, like every one else's hymn-book, I speak of your glory: 'A Collection of Hymns for the Use of the People called Methodists. By the Rev. John Wesley, M.A., sometime Fellow of Lincoln College, Oxford. With a supplement. London: Wesleyan Conference Office, 2 Castle Street, City Road; sold at 66 Paternoster Row.' That *was* a title page.[1] It had English history and English life in it, enough at least to set one bored little boy wondering. 'Fellow of Lincoln College, Oxford': so even at Caistor we had some touch with Oxford; but what Oxford was, I had no notion. I suppose I respect and love Oxford more than I should otherwise because I first heard of it in a Methodist hymn-book. 'Sometime Fellow of Lincoln College.' What was a Fellow and a sometime Fellow? And why *Lincoln* College?—a pertinent question in Lincolnshire. And then, opposite the title page—surely in almost every one of the old books—there was what ought never to have been removed from any of them, the page of thicker paper with the clean-cut, chaste engraving of the venerable man himself, and his clear, beautiful signature, *John Wesley*. It was in itself an introduction to the engraver's art, for it was a good engraving; and early familiarity with that dignified figure—the long curling hair, the Geneva gown and cassock and bands—gave me, I imagine, my ineradicable prejudice in favour of a properly dressed minister and my revulsion from the parson in mufti. Did it do no more? It did, and you made one of the profoundest mistakes you ever made when in 1904 you removed that engraving from your hymn-books.

[1] The edition of the hymn-book which I describe in this paper is not the classical one of 1780, but an undated mid-nineteenth-century edition (used by my grandfather), with the 1830 supplement.

That engraving alone stamped on the mind and heart of your people the figure of the founder of Methodism. Your devotion to him has been a by-word with the rest of us, you know, since Crabbe wrote of you as folk whose 'John the Elder was the John Divine'.

Well, let Crabbe have his joke: I think Methodism will lose a most valuable and most characteristic bit of itself when the lineaments of its founder are less clear in the mind of all its people. Every Methodist ought to know at least what Wesley looked like: and you began to erase his image when you removed him from the book. Why you did so wanton and so silly a thing, I cannot imagine. Yes, I can; but I will not go into that.

So much we learnt from the first opening of the book. Now turn over. A single page of close print contained the Preface, signed like the portrait, *John Wesley*, and dated (how many of you know the date?) London, October 20, 1779; a great but unobserved Methodist feast. I am inclined to read the whole of the Preface to you; for, unwilling as I am to think ill of you, I believe that many of you have never read it. Never read it! Why, you have never seen it. The rascals who compiled your hymn-book in 1904 saw to that. They had the effrontery to refer to it as 'a celebrated preface' ('*a* preface' forsooth); and the wickedness to banish it from the book which you were to use for thirty years. They robbed you in 1904 of what, as the children of John Wesley, you should regard as one of your priceless heirlooms. I use strong language, but that Preface is, to begin with, one of the noblest pieces of eighteenth-century prose extant: from its quaint opening words, 'For many years I have been importuned', to its moving conclusion, 'When Poetry thus keeps its place, as the handmaid of Piety, it shall attain, not a poor perishable wreath, but a crown that fadeth not away'. I used to read it often; I do not say I understood it then; but because I read it first in Caistor chapel I have kept on reading it till I begin to understand it. Apart altogether from Methodist interest, it is a first-rate introduction to the mind of the eighteenth century, a stimulating bit of literary criticism, and a model of plain, forceful, and at times sarcastic prose. I shall return to the Preface, but let us now pass on.

The Table of Contents follows. It is, of course, unique. Wesley said, 'The hymns are not carelessly jumbled together, but carefully ranged under proper heads, according to the experience of real Christians'. The arrangement is quite unlike that with which we are now all familiar: hymns, I mean, arranged as they are in almost all our books under the three main heads: God, the Father, the Son, and the Holy Ghost; Man, his needs and moods; the Church, its privileges and services. Wesley arranged his hymn-book as a spiritual biography of the sort of person whom he called in the Preface a real Christian. There is the introductory section, 'Exhorting sinners to return to God'; followed by a contemplation of the great facts which should induce them to do so: the Pleasantness of Religion, the Goodness of God, and the last four things, Death, Judgement, Heaven, and Hell. Next, the outlines of religion being sketched for the contemplation of the Exhorted Sinner, Formal Religion is described and distinguished (in Part II) from Inward Religion. With this precaution taken, the real work begins in Part III. Here we have the sinner trying to find the light. He prays for repentance in Section I. In Section II he is already a mourner convinced of sin. He is on the sure way to become a believer. But stay; before we deal with the sinner turned believer, we must glance at another class. Not all those who pray for repentance and wish to begin the true life do it now for the first time. Some have been here before, have started well, then have failed, and by this time need to get their second wind, or, it may be, their third or fourth. These are the people delightfully called Backsliders. And so we have the two sections: 'For Persons convinced of Backsliding' and 'For Backsliders recovered'. Wesley now sees his way clear. He has put the saving facts before sinners; warned them against mistaking false religion for true; and brought them to genuine repentance, whether for the first or a later time. He can now pass on to consider their experience as believers. He contemplates them first rejoicing, then fighting, praying, watching, working, suffering, seeking full redemption—a long and most distinctive section—and then saved; finally interceding for the world. In the last section Wesley considers his Society (the Methodist Church, as we should now call it); and we have the hymns of corporate life: For the Society Meeting, Giving Thanks, Praying, and Parting.

With the history of the various supplements I do not propose to deal. In them we find the beginning of the more usual present-day grouping of hymns. They contain, of course, some of the greatest of Charles Wesley's hymns at first published separately; we find here in particular some of the sacramental hymns and the hymns for the great festivals. Into the very canon approved by John Wesley his followers did not hesitate, however, to insert a few not inserted in his life; but they marked these evidences of their rash piety by branding these pirate hymns with an asterisk. Most famous of these is 'Jesu, Lover of My Soul'.[1] In 1830 the compilers confess that some of the hymns which they now admit 'sink below the rank of the Wesley poetry', but they defend their inclusion of these because of 'some excellence which will be found in the sentiment', because they afford a greater choice of subjects, and because 'Mr. Wesley' himself gave most of them his sanction by putting them in smaller supplemental books of his own.

Before we look into the hymns themselves, we must glance at the end of the book. Here is a mass of indexes:[2] indexes which by their thoroughness and minuteness link the book with Medieval and Renaissance scholarship. Scholars had not yet forgotten the way to index a book when Wesley published his hymns, and so we have a variety of indexes, which show that the book was used, as he intended it to be used, as 'a little body of experimental and practical divinity'. There is an excellent index of subjects—not an apology for one, but the genuine article, of great use to any user of the book. There is

[1] Included in *Hymns and Spiritual Songs*, 1753, but not in the hymn-book of 1780.

[2] The index of subjects and the index of texts were added in 1808.

an index of texts of Holy Scripture illustrated in the volume. This is not complete, it goes without saying, for there is a reminiscence of Holy Scripture in every verse, almost in every line, that Charles Wesley ever wrote. But, necessarily incomplete as it is, this index proves how fully justified was John Wesley's suggestion that in no other publication of the kind could men discover 'so distinct and full an account of Scriptural Christianity'. Of the thirty-nine books of the Old Testament, only four are not recorded as illustrated: Ezra, Obadiah, Nahum, and Zephaniah. Of the twenty-seven books of the New Testament, only one: the Third Epistle of St. John. Some books, e.g. Romans and Isaiah, are illustrated chapter by chapter, almost verse by verse. There are, for instance, over thirty references to Romans viii. Last among indexes there is the Index to every verse: giving evidence, if there were no other, that the book was used for reference and study. The book is indeed a treasury for the expression of every state of mind and every condition of the soul. It is a modern Book of Psalms. Exactly as the devout of all times have found in the Psalms a better expression of their fears and hopes, their defeats and victories, than in any words they could put together for themselves, so the lover of Wesley's hymns finds inevitably and unconsciously that he drops into quoting them whatever point he has to make, whatever confession he has to utter. Before we look at the hymns themselves, then, I want to emphasize to you the unique possession of your Church in this book which you hardly know to-day. You talk much, and you talk rightly, of the work Methodism does for the world and for the universal Church; but your greatest—incomparably your greatest—contribution to the common heritage of Christendom is in Wesley's hymns. All the other things which you do, others have done and can do as well, better, or less well. But in Wesley's hymns you have something unique, no one else could have done it, and unless you preserve it for the use of all the faithful, till that day when we are all one, we shall all lose some of the best gifts of God. I implore you then, in these days when you are tempted

to look at other parts of the Church and to dwell on your like-
ness to them and on the great things that we all have in common,
keep that good thing committed peculiarly to your charge. This
is your vineyard: do not come one day saying, 'Whatever I have
done elsewhere, mine own vineyard have I not kept'. In
Wesley's hymns, not divorced from the great tunes of the
Handel tradition, you have what only you understand and what
(I sometimes fear) you no longer think it worth while to
understand.

You may think my language about the hymns extravagant:
therefore I repeat it in stronger terms. This little book—some
750 hymns[1]—ranks in Christian literature with the Psalms, the
Book of Common Prayer, the Canon of the Mass. In its own
way, it is perfect, unapproachable, elemental in its perfection.
You cannot alter it except to mar it; it is a work of supreme
devotional art by a religious genius. You may compare it with
Leonardo's 'Last Supper' or King's Chapel; and, as Blackstone
said of the English Constitution, the proper attitude to take to
it is this: we must venerate where we are not able presently to
comprehend.

If you are now in a fit state of mind, we will look at the
hymns. Let me admit at once that, in spite of all I have said,
Charles Wesley did not always write well. The book contains
many stilted, feeble, dull verses, and not a few that may strike
us as ludicrous. These weaknesses are especially to be noticed
when Wesley writes of occasional or less exalted subjects.
Among the hymns included under the heading 'For Believers
Interceding' are, for instance, some 'For Masters'. These are
interesting inasmuch as they give us the point of view of an
eighteenth-century householder with his apprentices, his servants, and his family around him:

> Inferiors, as a sacred trust,
>   I from the Sovereign Lord receive,
> That what is suitable and just,
>   Impartial I to all may give:

[1] Wesley's Collection of 1780 has only 525 hymns.

O'erlook them with a guardian eye;
    From vice and wickedness restrain;
Mistakes and lesser faults pass by,
    And govern with a looser rein.

The servant faithfully discreet,
    Gentle to him, and good, and mild,
Him would I tenderly entreat,
    And scarce distinguish from a child.

Yet let me not my place forsake,
    The occasion of his stumbling prove,
The servant to my bosom take,
    Or mar him by familiar love.

As far from abjectness as pride,
    With condescending dignity,
Jesus, I make Thy word my guide,
    And keep the post assign'd by Thee.

That you may think merely quaint; but it is much to be wished that all modern employers read on to the last two verses:

O could I emulate the zeal
    Thou dost to Thy poor servants bear!
The troubles, griefs, and burdens feel
    Of souls entrusted to my care:

In daily prayer to God commend
    The souls whom God expired to save:
And think how soon my sway may end
    And all be equal in the grave!

The hymns 'For Parents' show some concern lest the rod be too much spared, and the child spoilt.

We tremble at the danger near,
    And crowds of wretched parents see
Who, blindly fond, their children rear
    In tempers far as hell from Thee:

> Themselves the slaves of sense and praise,
>   Their babes who pamper and admire,
> And make the helpless infants pass
>   To murderer Moloch through the fire.

Parents are to be concerned rather—

> To time our every smile or frown,
>   To mark the bounds of good and ill,
> And beat the pride of nature down,
>   And bend or break his rising will.

And again, in another hymn:

> We plunge ourselves in endless woes,
>   Our helpless infant sell;
> Resist the light, and side with those
>   Who send their babes to hell.

> We mark the idolizing throng,
>   Their cruel fondness blame;
> Their children's souls we know they wrong;—
>   And we shall do the same.

Yet parents may hope to avoid extreme measures:

> We would persuade their heart t' obey;
>   With mildest zeal proceed;
> And never take the harsher way,
>   When love will do the deed.

The hymn 'For the Mahometans' has great interest for students of Church history. Wesley has given a vivid and a true picture of the devastation wrought in the Christian East by Islam. He displays a sympathetic appreciation of the facts remarkable for his time when English Christians were perhaps even less understanding about the tragedy of the Eastern Church than we are to-day. This hymn alone would mark the extra-ordinarily wide and understanding survey which the Wesleys made of the Christian world; it was not an idle boast, that of John's: 'I look upon the whole world as my parish.' The two brothers had the most truly Catholic mind in eighteenth-century England—nay, in eighteenth-century Christendom:

> The smoke of the infernal cave,
>   Which half the Christian world o'erspread,
> Disperse, Thou heavenly Light, and save
>   The souls by that Impostor led,
> That Arab-chief, as Satan bold,
>   Who quite destroy'd Thy Asian fold.

> O might the blood of sprinkling cry
>   For those who spurn the sprinkled blood!
> Assert Thy glorious Deity,
>   Stretch out Thine arm, Thou Triune God!
> The Unitarian fiend expel,
>   And chase his doctrine back to hell.

The couplet about the Unitarian fiend has perhaps a wider application than to Mahometans; as I have sometimes wondered in old days if Wesley did not write with a prophet's pen that couplet about a widely circulated religious weekly:

> The world, *The Christian World*, convince
>   Of damning unbelief.

I know not how it is among you, but many well-meaning Congregationalists, I am sorry to say, are now too well-bred, or too squeamish, to sing that great missionary hymn of Heber's, in which we can breathe again the fervent faith of the heroic days of modern missions. I mean, of course, 'From Greenland's icy mountains'. How then would they get on with Wesley: 'For the Heathen'?

> The servile progeny of Ham
>   Seize, as the purchase of Thy blood;
> Let all the Heathens know Thy name;
>   From idols to the living God
> The dark Americans convert;
>   And shine in every Pagan heart.

There are, of course, quaint passages in the main body of hymns:

> Me, me who still in darkness sit,
>   Shut up in sin and unbelief,
> Bring forth out of this hellish pit,
>   This dungeon of despairing grief.

> Suffice that for the season past
>   Hell's horrid language fill'd our tongues;
> We all Thy words behind us cast,
>   And loudly sang the drunkard's songs.

There are references to the contemporary controversy with the Calvinists. Were the benefits of the Atonement intended for the whole race or only for those who did in fact receive them? Here is a hymn which sounds to-day as if any one might sing it; but in Wesley's time it was a battle-song of militant Arminianism. Notice the stab at debased Calvinism in every line:

> Father, whose everlasting love
>   Thy only Son for sinners gave;
> Whose grace to all did freely move,
>   And sent Him down the world to save:

> Help us Thy mercy to extol,
>   Immense, unfathom'd, unconfined;
> To praise the Lamb who died for all,
>   The general Saviour of mankind.

> Thy undistinguishing regard
>   Was cast on Adam's fallen race;
> For all Thou hast in Christ prepared
>   Sufficient, sovereign, saving grace.

The world He suffer'd to redeem:
　For all He hath th' atonement made:
For those that will not come to Him,
　The ransom of His life was paid.

Arise, O God, maintain Thy cause!
　The fulness of the Gentiles call:
Lift up the standard of Thy cross,
　And all shall own Thou diedst for all.

It is time to leave these curiosities and turn to the central part of the book. Why do I confidently make such great claims for it? Well, first a word about the language and literary form. It was Charles Wesley's good fortune, or (if you like) it was in the providence of God, that he was set to express the Catholic faith as it was being newly received in the Evangelical movement at a moment when prevailing taste and prevailing literary habits combined to give him a perfect literary instrument for hymn-writing. Dryden, Pope, and the rest of the much derided 'Classical' school had just shown what could be done with the English language inside the limits of what Milton called 'the troublesome and modern bondage of riming'.

Charles Wesley's generation was bred to the use of rhymed couplets and formal metres as you to-day are bred to the control of cars and wireless sets. In trying to say what he had to say in common metre, long metre, short metre, 6.8s, 7s and 6s, 8s and 6s, and the like, he was not kicking against the pricks as the genius of Francis Thompson or Christina Rossetti would have been. He was moving naturally in what was to him a natural medium, and so you simply are not aware of the trammels of the literary form, because he is not. He moves with complete mastery, with an ease that conceals mastery. His art is so cunning that it is difficult indeed to illustrate it.

We are, however, all aware of odd jolts that we get in some hymns where the sense quarrels with the metre or oversteps it. That very literary person, F. S. Pierpoint, in his exquisite (I use the adjective in its good *and* its bad sense) hymn, 'For the

Beauty of the Earth', though he is rather oppressively 'cultured' most of the time, is not master of his metre and crashes awkwardly in verse two:

> For the beauty of each hour
> Of the day and of the night.

You don't want to emphasize the absurd word 'of', but Pierpoint has contrived his couplet so ill that you must.

Or we may look at Tennyson (though this is not quite fair, because Tennyson was not writing a hymn). The opening stanzas of *In Memoriam* make a noble hymn; but there is that metrical difficulty (apart from discovering exactly what Tennyson means) in the last stanzas:

> Let knowledge grow from more to more,
>   But more of reverence in us dwell,
>   That heart and mind, according well,
> May make one music as before,
>
> But vaster. We are fools and slight.

But vaster is an awkward 'carry over' to a new verse and a new start of the tune. It is a great merit in a hymn if each line, to say nothing of each verse, contains a more or less rounded thought. I dare say that you have often felt that in singing the great hymn of Dr. Watts on which John Wesley died, 'I'll praise my Maker'. It goes smoothly enough till you come to—

> Happy the man whose hopes rely
> On Israel's God! He made the sky,
>   And earth and seas, with all their train.

I know that it is partly the Psalmist's fault. Watts was following him, and the Psalmist has this sudden transition: 'He made the sky'; but it would have been neater, nevertheless, if Watts had made the transition in meaning at the end of the line where you get the natural transition of metre. And what I am driving at is that Charles Wesley never, or almost never, is caught out by his metre as Pierpoint and Watts and Tennyson (considered as a hymn-writer) are; and as almost every one is. There may be examples in Wesley: I can only say that I have noticed none. His strong accent always seems to fall in the right place; and most lines contain one thought and not more than one.

You do not notice his perfect mastery of his medium, I said; but you can trace it. To do that helps to explain the smoothness of his verse and his success in bringing it off every time with a facility which, at its worst, is almost a sort of slickness. I will give you one example. You know the literary artifice called by the grammarians 'chiasmus'. You have four ideas which hang together in two pairs, which we can call A and B. Instead of dealing first with the first pair, the A's and then with the B's, you mention one of the first pair, then both the second pair, and then finish with the second member of the first pair: A B B A. There sounds to be little in it, but it is most effective, especially in four lines of verse. Let us look at a hymn in detail. Take the great baptismal hymn, 'Come Father, Son, and Holy Ghost'. You remember verse two:

> We now Thy promised presence claim,
>   Sent to disciple all mankind,
>   Sent to baptize into Thy Name,
> We now Thy promised presence find.

You have there the lines 1 and 4 similar and the lines 2 and 3 similar. You see how Wesley rings the changes. Beginning with *promised presence*, he goes off to the idea of *Sent to do* this; then he presses that home again, *Sent to do* that; and finally gives the knock-out blow by a return to the place from which he started, *promised presence*.

Now take a hymn like 'Jesu, Lover', about which I dare say you think you know everything. Here Wesley's feeling is very high. You know this hymn is often criticized as poor in literary form, though moving in its piety. Many jests have been made about the confused navigation pictured in the metaphors of verse one: a bosom in a storm becomes a ship; and our Saviour, from being the pilot ('safely to the haven guide') is turned into some one on the shore who welcomes the vessel. That sort of comment is all very small and silly; I mention it only to show that, even in a hymn where Wesley's control of his metaphors is not the tightest, he still is very active with his quiet skill of weaving a pattern in his words. Consider the famous verse that brings divine consolation to millions who never think of its literary form. Have you noticed the finger-prints of the accomplished classical scholar still on that?

> Just and holy is Thy Name,
>   I am all unrighteousness;
> False and full of sin I am,
>   Thou art full of truth and grace.

Here you have two people in contrast: the holy Saviour and the sinful speaker. Wesley begins with the Saviour. 'Just and holy is Thy Name'; then he has two lines on the sinful speaker:

> I am all unrighteousness;
> False and full of sin I am.

And, finally, he mentions the Saviour again: 'Thou art full of truth and grace.'

The contrast, that is to say, is made two ways in the first two lines: Saviour—sinner; then in the next two, sinner—Saviour: A B B A. But look at the pattern of the verse a little more closely. Inside this main design you see two variants of it worked, so to say, on a smaller scale. Take the lines about the sinner:

> I am all unrighteousness:
> False and full of sin I am.

Here you have the pronoun 'I' and a description of the speaker, 'I am all unrighteousness': 'I am false and full of sin'. But you see how Wesley arranges it: 'I' first, then epithet: 'I am all unrighteousness'; then comes another epithet, and lastly 'I': 'False and full of sin I am'. A B B A.

Now look at the two lines about the Saviour. They exactly balance; and the same literary device is used in precisely the same way.

> Just and holy is Thy Name; A B
>
> Thou art full of truth and grace. B A

So in four very simple lines, on the most simple theme, we have the same effective pattern twice woven small, and then the whole enclosed in a larger setting of exactly the same pattern.

This, I know, has been tedious, and perhaps not very convincing. I must mention it, however, because it gives you a hint of the literary power and skill and instinct for form that lie behind Wesley's success as a verse maker. I must not analyse more. If he does that in four comparatively simple lines, you may judge what he does elsewhere. *Ex pede Herculem.* I do not suggest that Methodist congregations know why the verse is good; but if it is good and clear, and not tedious and flat, it is so, I submit, because your congregations unconsciously benefit by Wesley's literary power. And it was, as I said, Wesley's good fortune that the sort of literary skill most appreciated in his day, and therefore that in which he was most trained, was a skill which helped him in writing the concise verse that is necessary in hymns. After the Romantic Revival, another kind of verse—of a more continuous, straggling kind—came into fashion; and when it was chopped into verses, it often seemed, and indeed it was, unnatural and unhappy.

But it was not only in the form of his metre that Wesley was happy. He lived in an age of robust common sense, common sense that was often pedestrian and uninspiring and commonplace, but common sense for all that. This gave his language a clarity and reality and vigour that are most precious. For in religion, if it is to save souls (or whatever the modern phrase may be), those qualities—clarity, reality, vigour—are essential. In religious talk you must understand what the fellow means; you must be sure he is talking about facts and talking sincerely; you must be knocked down, or at least effectually persuaded, by what he says. Now, of all people who talk about religion, Charles Wesley is the least sentimental and soulful. There is no sort of self-conscious tension or priggishness or humbug about him. He says what he has to say in the simplest, plainest way he can. He does not take refuge in abstract nouns and over-subtle adjectives. Concrete nouns, active verbs, and plain metaphors: these are his material. He can use a Latin word on occasion with great effect. At times he can be so scholarly as to be hardly understood by the crowd. But these are quite exceptional moods; and he is *never* foggy. His allusions sometimes may be too erudite for most to grasp; but, once grasped, they are quite simple. Take these examples—space permits only sample verse quotations:

> Arm of the Lord, awake, awake!
>   Thine own immortal strength put on!
> With terror clothed, hell's kingdom shake,
>   And cast Thy foes with fury down.
>
> As in the ancient days appear!
>   The sacred annals speak Thy fame:
> Be now omnipotently near,
>   To endless ages still the same.
>
> Thy arm, Lord, is not shorten'd now;
>   It wants not now the power to save;
> Still present with Thy people, thou
>   Bear'st them through life's disparted wave.
>
> Where pure, essential joy is found,
>   The Lord's redeem'd their heads shall raise,
> With everlasting gladness crown'd,
>   And fill'd with love, and lost in praise.

You will notice how full this is of scriptural allusion: in places it is almost a transcript from scripture. You will notice its vigour, its simple metaphors, its occasional Latin, '*omnipotently near*', 'pure *essential* joy'.

> When Israel out of Egypt came,
>   And left the proud oppressor's land,
> Supported by the great *I Am*,
>   Safe in the hollow of His hand,
> The Lord in Israel reign'd alone,
> And Judah was His favourite throne.
>
> Creation, varied by His hand,
>   Th' omnipotent Jehovah knows;
> The sea is turn'd to solid land,
>   The rock into a fountain flows;
> And all things, as they change, proclaim
> The Lord eternally the same.

Here is an extreme example of Wesley's more erudite verse (he is speaking of Heaven):

> Those amaranthine bowers
> (Unalienably ours)
> Bloom, our infinite reward,
>   Rise, our permanent abode;
> From the founded world prepared;
>   Purchased by the blood of God.

'Amaranthine bowers' and 'the founded world' need footnotes; but little of Wesley is like that. On the other hand, it is pleasant to find with how sure a touch he deals with a technical subject like heraldry, as he does in the verse:

> What though a thousand hosts engage,
>   A thousand worlds, my soul to shake?
> I have a shield shall quell their rage,
>   And drive the alien armies back;
> Portray'd it bears a bleeding Lamb:
> I dare believe in Jesu's name.

Portray'd is a word that betrays the man who knows how to
describe a shield.

This use of simple, direct words is illustrated by the Table
of Contents. Where modern editors talk in long Latin abstract
nouns, regeneration, temptation, discipline, resignation, aspiration, consecration, Welsey hits out simply: 'For Believers
fighting, suffering, praying.'

This gift of elemental simplicity and stinging direct speech
comes out in such a hymn as that for the Watch Night Service,
'Come, let us anew'. I know not how it is with you, but
familiarity has never made me proof against the sheer magic
of the words:

> Our life is a dream;
> Our time, as a stream,
> Glides swiftly away;
> And the fugitive moment refuses to stay.

> The arrow is flown;
> The moment is gone;
> The millennial year
> Rushes on to our view, and eternity's here.

Notice the supreme cunning which introduces into the simple
Anglo-Saxon the two Latin adjectives, the *fugitive* moment,
the *millennial* year.

But all this, you will say (and you will say very truly), does
not suffice to make the book great, religiously great. I agree.
So far I have spoken only of the external things because I want
you to see those, as I saw them, first. That was not first which
is spiritual, but that which is natural. Wesley might have done
all that I have mentioned so far, and yet have been no more
than one of those competent versifiers with whom the eighteenth
century abounded. His precise verse and his simple, unaffected
language, had there been nothing behind them, would have produced a book edifying indeed, but dull and unmoving. We have
to inquire, therefore, what *was* behind. What made Wesley
different from the pious poetasters of his generation—different

as the Canon of the Mass is different from modern Romanist handbooks of devotion, different (that is to say) by the whole difference of religious genius? I will name three things among the many which might be named.

First, there is the full-orbed and conscious orthodoxy of a scholar trained and humbled as he contemplates the holy, catholic, and evangelical faith in its historic glory and strength. The hymns are charged with dogma. They set forth, not the amiable generalizations of natural religion in which Wesley's contemporaries delighted, but the peculiar and pungent doctrines of uncompromising Christianity. References to the doctrine of the Holy Trinity, of the Incarnation, of Redemption by the Passion, of the Resurrection—we never move far from these. Simply to state the doctrine of the Holy Trinity is for Wesley a pleasure and a means of grace. Often he wants nothing more than that: it is enough for him to name the Name of God:

> Round us when we speak Thy Name
> There spreads a heaven of light.

This quality in his work puts Wesley in line with the greatest hymn-writers of the Greek Church. A most prominent feature in their hymns, as in his, is the spiritual exaltation which they discover as they glory in a statement of the orthodox faith and as they triumphantly assert the Christian doctrine of God. Hear Wesley on the Incarnation:

> Let earth and heaven combine,
>   Angels and men agree,
> To praise in songs divine
>   The incarnate Deity;
> Our God contracted to a span,
> Incomprehensibly made man.
>
> He laid His glory by,
>   He wrapp'd Him in our clay,
> Unmark'd by human eyes,
>   The latent Godhead lay;
> Infant of days He here became,
> And bore the mild Immanuel's name.

Hear him on the Passion:

> With glorious clouds encompas't round,
>   Whom angels dimly see,
> Will the Unsearchable be found,
>   Or God appear to me?
>
> Jehovah in Thy person show,
>   Jehovah crucified!
> And then the pardoning God I know,
>   And feel the blood applied.

Wesley's orthodoxy, it is true, some of your modern theologians have been rash enough to question. With puny daring, they suggest that he denies the true humanity of the Son and flirts with patripassianism. This is a feeble and unconvincing display by men who wince before the strength of his doctrine. Let them master the doctrine of the communication of attributes, as Wesley mastered it, and fears for his orthodoxy will give place to fears for their own. It is, then, because Wesley has such great things to say—stupendous assertions about God made Man—that in his hands the slick mechanical metres of the eighteenth century are not only smooth and easy, but moving and even harrowing.

But Wesley, as probably he does not quite reach the excellence of the Greek writers in dogmatic hymns, goes beyond them in another way. For Wesley has not only the full faith to set out; he goes on to tell of a present experience, of its effects in his own life:

> What we have felt and seen
> With confidence we tell.

Most men and women merely disgust us when they talk about their souls and their secret experiences; they did this quite effectually even before psychology became the rage; but Wesley's common sense and scholarly taste kept him from mawkish excesses without crushing his spirit. The result is that few people have been as successful as he was in speaking at once with passion and with decency about God's work in their own lives. For him the important things are the great, external, objective truths about God, the Father, the Son, and the Holy Ghost, and the definite impact of faith in these on his own life and other men's. Through all the book there rings an absolutely overmastering note of confidence, certainty, and happiness. 'The best of all is, God is with us', with us especially in Emmanuel, the incarnate Son: nothing can make Wesley forget that. Historic Christianity applied to the individual soul and the sharing of this experience with other men who know it too —so Wesley reaches that sense of a common life which all 'real' Christians—Wesley's word—live. So, too, he comes to yearn over the great troubled world that is missing this heavenly treasure.

Lastly, there is something else. There is the solid structure of historic dogma; there is the passionate thrill of present experience; but there is, too, the glory of a mystic sunlight coming directly from another world. This transfigures history and experience. This puts past and present into the timeless eternal now. This brings together God and man until Wesley talks with God as a man talks with his friend. This gives to the hymn-book its divine audacity, those passages only to be understood by such as have sat in heavenly places in Christ Jesus, and being caught up into paradise have heard unspeakable words which it is not lawful for a man to utter.

Let me illustrate this mystical quality by two of the most famous hymns. In them Wesley is at the height of his inspiration: nothing short of inspiration keeps the daring emotion sane and reverent and orthodox. The first is:

> Ah! show me that happiest place,
>   The place of Thy people's abode,
> Where saints in an ecstasy gaze,
>   And hang on a crucified God;
> Thy love for a sinner declare,
>   Thy passion and death on the tree;
> My spirit to Calvary bear,
>   To suffer and triumph with Thee.

The second example is, of course, 'Wrestling Jacob', that hymn described with such power by Percy Lubbock in his account of Dr. Warre's sermons in Eton Chapel. Wesley saw in this story of Jacob prevailing over the mysterious Wrestler even under the old dispensation a mystical revelation of the humiliation of the Word; and he argues, commands, and hectors as if the Word of God were already wearing our Flesh. I should like to quote it all; I will remind you only of it:

> Come, O Thou Traveller unknown,
> Whom still I hold, but cannot see!

Incidentally, we notice those doctrines that Barth is teaching us anew in the lines:

> When I am weak, then I am strong;
> And when my all of strength shall fail,
> I shall with the God-Man prevail.

There have been other writers of dogmatic hymns (we think of the Greek Church); there have been other writers of hymns revealing a personal experience of religion (we think of the nineteenth century); there have been other writers of mystical religious poetry (we think of the seventeenth century). It is Wesley's glory that he united these three strains—dogma, experience, mysticism—in verse so simple that it could be understood, and so smooth that it could be used, by plain men. You can find a union of these qualities in the greatest Latin hymns of the Medieval Church, but hardly (I believe) anywhere else.

These three qualities, among others, give such a life to the hymns that they can never grow old while Christians experience God's grace. There is indeed a strange timelessness about them: their essential confidence does not rest on the position won by the gospel at the time of Wesley's writing, on the progress or lack of progress of the work of God. Some few of the expressions are such as we should not use to-day, but the main things that Wesley has to say we want still to say. He is greatest when he is on the greatest things; greatest of all, possibly, in his sacramental hymns. In reading fully one which your modern book truncates, I end. Notice its simple language, its profound and vigorous orthodoxy, its firm personal faith and experience, its mystical air:

> Victim Divine, Thy grace we claim,
>   While thus Thy precious death we show:
> Once offer'd up a spotless Lamb.
>   In Thy great temple here below,
> Thou didst for all mankind atone,
> And standest now before the throne.
>
> Thou standest in the holy place,
>   As now for guilty sinners slain;
> The blood of sprinkling speaks, and prays,
>   All prevalent for helpless man;
> Thy blood is still our ransom found,
> And speaks salvation all around.
>
> The smoke of Thy atonement here
>   Darken'd the sun, and rent the veil,
> Made the new way to heaven appear,
>   And show'd the great Invisible;
> Well pleased in Thee, our God look'd down,
> And calls His rebels to a crown.
>
> He still respects Thy sacrifice;
>   Its savour sweet doth always please:
> The Offering smokes through earth and skies,
>   Diffusing life, and joy, and peace;
> To these, Thy lower courts, it comes,
> And fills them with divine perfumes.
>
> We need not now go up to heaven,
>   To bring the long-sought Saviour down;
> Thou art to all already given,
>   Thou dost even now Thy banquet crown:
> To every faithful soul appear,
> And show Thy real presence here!

THE RECALL TO RELIGION IN THE HYMNS
OF CHARLES WESLEY

In the last years of the War and the first years of the peace, Arthur Christopher Benson was Master of Magdalene. He lived, not in the new Lodge, but in the old Lodge in Magdalene Street, a house turned now into sets of rooms. It was my good fortune to be one of the many on whom he showered kindnesses, and often in those years I used to call on him and go out with him walking or bicycling. You rang a bell at the street door, and after a rather long delay you were admitted: not, as you at first expected, to the house, but to a short cloister open on one side and leading to a french window. Before you passed through the french window, you often heard the comfortable notes of organ music proceeding in a smothered sort of fashion from an inner room. The french window admitted you to an outer hall, dark with tapestry and crowded with pictures; from it you entered an inner waiting-room, sandwiched (as you learnt later) between the Master's study and his bedroom. This room looked out on the Master's garden. It was lighted by windows partly filled with quaint Dutch painted glass of the seventeenth century. In this inner waiting-room you found the Master playing, with apparent carelessness and with infinite satisfaction, a small organ.

What was he playing? Well, as often as not, Charles Wesley's hymns to such tunes as *Stella;* and, if you glanced round the room you saw at least half a score of busts and images of the great John himself. Benson was the son of an archbishop, but he had been a boy in Lincoln Chancery and a young man in Methodist Cornwall; and in those congenial atmospheres he had acquired, as he often told me, a devotion to the Wesleys. To be sure, he treated them as disrespectfully as he treated every one else of whom he was fond. He dissected, criticized, mocked at, and misunderstood them with conscious but entertaining perversity.

Nevertheless, he returned to them with affection and veneration, and he liked nothing better than to play these hymns and to quote them.

As I used to go into that dark and slightly mysterious house and hear the familiar tunes, I got many and many a time the feeling that something had assured me of the unshaken truth of essential Christianity. Those years of war were years of much argument, much questioning, much doubt, much despair; but to hear the tunes which cried out the words of Wesley's faith was, at least for me, to feel myself confirmed mysteriously in the faith itself. Why this happened no doubt any fifth-rate psychologist could explain. Those tunes and (to use one of Wesley's favourite expressions) the latent words I had first known and had unforgettably learnt in the remote Lincolnshire wolds. The tunes and the faith still enjoyed the security, the certainty, that then were features of all my schoolboy life. Wesley's hymns to *Stella, Euphony, Sovereignty, Irish,* Justification by Faith, the Plan of Salvation, the Gift of God, the Wages of Sin, it was all as certain to recur on Sunday as the football match on Saturday, an illicit drive over the Wolds about every other week, the sheep fair in March, and the roundabouts in the Market Place in May. The plan of salvation and justification by faith were as much in the nature of things, as self-evident, and as much to be taken for granted as the benevolence of the Liberal party, the malevolence of the Conservatives, the wisdom of the minority on the Board of Guardians, and the iniquity of the local solicitors.

Yes, it all may be so. I think, nevertheless, that there was more in it than that; and to that I shall in due course return. Meanwhile I ask you to remember that sense of security as we take a look at the hymns themselves.

It will be difficult not to spend too much time over the form and structure: difficult especially for me who most Sunday nights in term endure *Hymns Ancient and Modern* with the wretched versification, doubtful grammar, and questionable theology thereof, much of it nowadays most appropriately set out in what I may call the jazz music of Vaughan Williams. Or, if we seek relief from *Ancient and Modern*, there is the *English Hymnal*, better it is true, but stuffed out with second-rate creaking translations of Greek and Latin hymns, fusty as a second-hand Lewis and Short, more like the meritorious exercises of the classical sixth than Poetry, the handmaid of Piety. Worst of all there is the self-conscious preciosity of *Songs of Praise*, mistaking quaintness for strength and antiquarianism for orthodoxy. From all such let us turn to Charles Wesley, and as we linger in the outer court let us notice, first, a simple but useful virtue which Wesley practises in almost every hymn. I mean that he binds his verses, not merely by rhyme, not merely by consecutive thought, but by verbal references which, without our noticing them, lead us from line to line. Wesley gives us no jumps in language to distract our attention from what he and we are saying. I choose a verse at random:

> Thou waitest to be gracious still;
> Thou dost with sinners bear,

the second *Thou* carries us on from the first:

> That, saved, we may Thy goodness feel,

we of this third line is *sinners* of line 2,

> And all Thy grace declare.

Thy grace, a repetition of the idea in *Thy goodness* of line 3.

It is the technique that the careful reader notes in Macaulay: every sentence is linked with the preceding sentence by a word or an allusion. This word or allusion throws the reader back to something which he has not had time to forget and so knits Macaulay's paragraph, like Wesley's verse, into one.

You value this fully if you have suffered from what I may call the ill-regulated verse of the next century: say, George Macdonald's morning prayer:

> Lord, let me live and act this day,
>   Still rising from the dead; [Why, *still*?]
> Lord, make my spirit good and gay—
>   Give me my daily bread.

Admirable sentiments, but a thought disconnected. The connexion between goodness and gaiety and rising from the dead needs looking for and exposing, if indeed it exists; whilst the connexion in thought between *daily bread* and what precedes seems to consist only in this: that *bread* rhymes undeniably with *dead*. It is the verse of a tyro: the verse that you and I write. I slide over the (to me) horrible posing childishness of praying to be gay. Wesley, I think, I hope, never descends to the triviality which pretends to be simplicity.

But let us compare Wesley with hymn-writers who were no tyros. In two writers at least in the nineteenth century we may perceive a mastery of the art of versification which excludes the grosser faults: Bishop Walsham How and Bishop Wordsworth at least knew that *of* is not a very good word on which to allow an accent to fall. Neither of them, we may think, would have written the shocking lines in that popular hymn of the Rabbi Felix Adler, 'Sing we of the golden city':

> It will pass into the splendours
>   Of the city of the light.

Let us see then what they can do.

Wordsworth can do well. 'Hark! the sound of holy voices' is honest verse and wholesome doctrine, even if its language is not so classically scriptural as Wesley's. But this is exceptionally good for Wordsworth. More often Wordsworth takes a scriptural metaphor and beats it out too thin in line after line, or, worse still, takes a metaphor of his own composing and does the same to it. He has a fatal facility for verse. He does not, like George Macdonald, have to think as far as *bread* to get a rhyme with *dead*; he gently expands every notion till it is sure sooner or later to rhyme with anything that may be about. Gospel light for Wordsworth does not merely glow: it glows with pure and radiant beams. Living water does not merely flow: it flows with soul-refreshing streams. The Bishop leaves nothing to the imagination. He drags out, shakes out, and ticks off every commonplace extension of every commonplace thought.

Until it was set to a feeble dance tune by Vaughan Williams, Bishop How's 'For all the saints' was a hymn with merit. It is perhaps a trifle too luscious and romantic to ring quite true for those of us whose human treasure is in fact in heaven. There is more than a touch of King Arthur and the Round Table about the distant triumph song, the golden evening brightening in the West, and Paradise the blest. But that is nothing. When we reach the last two verses, they ring dreadfully false and thin. The exactness of the geography of earth's bounds and ocean's coast does not fit the apocalyptic gates of pearl, and then with this unreal picture of the saints rising from land and sea and entering the gates of pearl we come suddenly on what should be no Arthurian romantic stuff: the doxology to the Holy Trinity. Compare this combination of Malory's tinsel and a young lady's water colour of a sunset with Wesley's virile presentation of the same communion of saints under the same metaphor of an army. I can scarcely bear not to quote it all, but you know it:

> One army of the living God,
>   To His command we bow;
> Part of His host have cross'd the flood,
>   And part are crossing now.
>
> His militant embodied host,
>   With wishful looks we stand;
> And long to see that happy coast,
>   And reach the heavenly land.

Not a word wasted. It is as spare and taut as the warriors it describes. Yet if more spare it is far more daring than How. Listen:

> Even now by faith we join our hands
>   With those that went before,
> And greet the blood-besprinkled bands
>   On the eternal shore.

There is a communion of saints indeed.

> Our spirits too shall quickly join,
>   Like theirs with glory crowned,
> And shout to see our Captain's sign,
>   To hear His trumpet sound.

If you want a military metaphor, that is it. No distant triumph song stealing in the ear or countless host streaming through gates of pearl, but—

> Shout to see our Captain's sign,
>   To hear His trumpet sound.

Not in vain for Wesley had Balaam prophesied: 'The Lord his God is with him; and the shout of a king is among them.'

If we study Wesley's use of metaphors and similes, we shall note that a very large proportion of them come directly from Holy Scripture or are reminiscences of Holy Scripture. John Wesley (you remember the Preface) praised his brother's hymns for their exposition of 'Scriptural Christianity'. The praise, of course, was merited, but might have been extended; in metaphor and simile, not less than in doctrine, Charles Wesley deserves that high and unfashionable commendation: *scriptural*. This constant reference to the classical language of the faith—the written Word of God—gives Charles Wesley's hymns themselves a classical poise and accent which marks them off, I believe, from all other modern hymns. It saves Wesley from the deplorable bathos and feeble amateurishness into which almost all other hymn-writers fall at times and from which some never escape. Great poetic genius is needed to use metaphor and simile in verse. Homer, Virgil, Milton can do it:

> Thick as autumnal leaves that strew the brooks
> In Vallombrosa,

and so on. But we ordinary folk, flying to metaphor and simile in our own strength, merely make ourselves ridiculous. Let me illustrate. The perfectly well-intentioned J. D. Burns attempts a metaphor of his own invention and at first fares pretty well:

> Thy ways are love—though they transcend
>   Our feeble range of sight,
> They wind through darkness to their end
>   In everlasting light.

But, encouraged, alas! by this success, he proceeds:

> Thy thoughts are love, and Jesus is
>   The loving voice they find;

Christ is indeed the Word, but what follows?

> His love lights up the vast abyss
>   Of the Eternal Mind.

We plunge from the sensible (I cannot say the sublime) to the ridiculous, perhaps indeed to the blasphemous. 'The vast abyss of the Eternal Mind' is not a reverent or a complimentary expression—even if you spell 'Eternal Mind' with capital letters and light it with a voice. That is what happens when a man of ordinary ability leaves the classical metaphors of Holy Scripture. Charles Wesley, who could do it with less risk than most hymn-writers, takes the risk less often than most. And when he does seem to me to have no scriptural authority, I believe that it is almost always because my knowledge of Holy Scripture is too exiguous to detect the reference.

I do not say that the non-scriptural metaphor always fails. Even the wishy-washy Faber succeeded with it once, in his one good hymn, because he kept it simple and short:

> Through life's long day and death's dark night,
> O gentle Jesus, be our light.

But for one success there are a thousand failures.

Baring Gould is a writer for whom, despite my better judgement, I have a sneaking affection, and 'Onward! Christian soldiers' is not to be written off hastily; but compare his treatment of a scriptural phrase with Wesley's treatment of the same phrase:

> Crowns and thrones may perish,
>   Kingdoms rise and wane,
> But the Church of Jesus
>   Constant will remain.
>
> Gates of hell can never
>   'Gainst that Church prevail;
> We have Christ's own promise
>   And that cannot fail.

How does Wesley say it? Before we read him, we may be sure he will avoid a bad stress like that in the last line 'And that cannot fail'. He will avoid the ugly ' 'gainst' and the needlessly emphatic '*that* Church', as if there were a multitude of churches. Notice the climbing effect of his verse. He saves his scripture till the last line; and boldly exaggerates the Gospel word from a negative resistance to a positive attack. Notice, too, the subtle use of alliteration: *w* in the first half of the verse, *m* in lines 5 and 6, *s* in lines 7 and 8.

> When He first the work begun,
> Small and feeble was His day:
> Now the word doth swiftly run,
> Now it wins its widening way;
> More and more it spreads and grows
> Ever mighty to prevail;
> Sin's strongholds it now o'erthrows,
> Shakes the trembling gates of hell.

The Gospel word *prevail* is wrested from the use of the gates of hell—the gates of hell shall not *prevail*—and the Church does not merely resist the gates, the prevailing word shakes them. It is the strong finish, all saved for a knock-out blow. Every verse of that superb hymn ends in such a line. All the preceding lines lead by steps to an emphatic concluding phrase.

Verse 1 ends:

> All partake the glorious bliss!

Verse 3 ends:

> Him Who spake a world from nought.

Verse 4 ends:

> All the Spirit of His love!

These other fellows appear at once as mere children and bunglers when we can, as here, compare their treatment of a theme with Wesley's treatment of the same theme.

I do not except Newman. 'Praise to the Holiest' is almost a great hymn. It has some very great verses; but you must have lamented over the feebleness of its ending. After presenting in awful language the theology of the sacrifice of Calvary, Newman ends as a Unitarian might have ended, as indeed a Unitarian did end, his Passion hymn. The second Adam, the higher gift than grace, God's Presence and His very Self—to what does it lead Newman? To this: the sacrifice of God Himself on the Cross is to teach us to bear suffering and death. True, no doubt; but what a perfect anti-climax! The Unitarian Martineau has it more passionately, for he can go as far as that:

> O Lord of sorrow, meekly die:
> Thou'lt heal or hallow all our woe,

and

> Great chief of faithful souls, arise,
> None else can lead the martyr-band.

It is not to the Roman Cardinal that we must look to supply the deficiencies of the Unitarian's faith. It is to one of ourselves, blessed be God. Hear Wesley:

Come, then, and to my soul reveal
 The heights and depths of grace,
The wounds which all my sorrows heal,
 That dear disfigured face.

Before my eyes of faith confest,
 Stand forth a slaughtered Lamb;
And wrap me in Thy crimson vest
 And tell me all Thy name.

Jehovah in Thy Person show,
 Jehovah crucified!
And then the pardoning God I know,
 And feel the blood applied.

I view the Lamb in His own light,
 Whom angels dimly see,
And gaze, transported at the sight,
 To all eternity.

Or this:

Endless scenes of wonder rise
 From that mysterious tree,
Crucified before our eyes,
 Where we our Maker see;
Jesus, Lord, what hast Thou done?
 Publish we the death divine,
Stop, and gaze, and fall, and own
 Was never love like Thine!

Never love nor sorrow was [Note that verbal link.]
 Like that my Saviour show'd:
See Him stretched on yonder Cross,
 And crushed beneath our load!
Now discern the Deity,
 Now His heavenly birth declare!
Faith cries out, 'Tis He, 'Tis He,
 My God, that suffers there!

Contrast Newman's mean conclusion:

> To teach His brethren, and inspire
> To suffer and to die.

Newman's is a humanitarian tinkling. Wesley's is the catholic, evangelical, orthodox, holy faith.

Here I must turn aside for a moment to triumph in Wesley's scholarship. To that we owe a feature of our eucharistic worship which neither the confused and truncated canon of the Roman Mass nor the Anglican rite has preserved. The epiclesis takes us back to the earliest and purest celebrations of the Supper of the Lord. This link with primitive catholicism which Rome and Canterbury threw away, Wesley restored.

> Come, Holy Ghost, Thine influence shed,
> And realize the sign.
> Thy life infuse into the bread,
> Thy power into the wine.

I need not quote more. Wesley gave us what Canterbury now struggles illegally to recover and what Rome stupidly lost in the Dark Ages and still rejects in these days of her wanton and self-conscious schism from ancient orthodoxy. We have almost nothing to learn even liturgically that we cannot learn from Wesley.

It is tempting, and you see that I cannot resist the temptation, to linger over the flawless forms of Wesley's hymns. Let us now move to consider two or three of the more obvious features of the content of the hymns. If you will suffer the paradox, we will begin by noting one feature that is not prominent. Last summer I read and re-read the whole of Isaac Watts's hymns. I seal my lips lest I begin to praise them, but I mention one quality which distinguishes them sharply from Wesley's. Watts, time and again, sets the faith of the Incarnation, the Passion, and the Resurrection against its cosmic background. He surveys the solar system, the planets, the fixed stars, the animal creation, from the beginning to the end of time.

He surveys the whole realm of Nature, as in an immortal phrase he has described it, and at the centre he always sees the dying and crucified Creator. Methodist editors have drawn freely on Watts to supply hymns of this type: I name only one, 'God is a Name my soul adores'. You remember it:

> A glance of Thine runs through the globe,
>   Rules the bright worlds, and moves their frame;

and so on. Methodists have borrowed these hymns to supplement Wesley, because Wesley had comparatively little to say on that subject. Wesley is obsessed with one theme: God and the Soul; for the stage in space and time on which that drama is set he has little concern. He is always at Calvary; no other place in the universe matters, and for him the course of historic time is lost in the eternal NOW. This is partly because of the urgent poignancy of his own evangelical experience. It is partly because his education, if more polished in classical form than Watts's, was less wide, less philosophical, less sweeping.

You find, therefore, that in the age of Deism Wesley is, of all writers, the least Deistic, the most uncompromisingly, the most exclusively Christian. There is little touch of 'Natural Religion' in Wesley. Do not misunderstand me. I do not charge Watts with Deism and Natural Religion. Watts, in that earlier generation, was near enough to the profound evangelicalism of seventeenth-century Calvinism to survey the whole realm of Nature and still to remain invincibly Christian; but fifty years later the experiment would have been more dangerous. It was perhaps well for Wesley that, in his more Deistic generation, he wore so constantly the blinkers that restricted his view to the essentials of the Christian faith. A cosmic view in his time was more difficult than in Watts's to combine with passionate orthodoxy.

We note then the exclusively Christian and New Testament

quality of Wesley's hymns. Truly he says of himself (accurate in every word):

> My heart is full of Christ, and longs
>   Its glorious matter to declare!
> Of Him I make my loftier songs,
>   I cannot from His praise forbear.

Take one rough, and not exhaustive, test. Of the 769 hymns in one edition not fewer than 84 have as their first word the Name: Jesus, Christ, or Saviour. One hymn in every nine *opens* so. In *Songs of Praise* the proportion is more like one in twenty-four. I have not gone a step lower, but I suspect that Wesley is one of the hymn-writers least well represented in Unitarian hymn-books.

You find in Wesley, therefore, comparatively few occasional hymns, for social, national, or human occasions. The index of your old hymn-book teaches you that. God and the Soul: 'clear directions for making your calling and election sure, for perfecting holiness in the fear of God'—this is Wesley's concern. We find Sinners exhorted, Mourners convinced of sin, Persons convinced of backsliding, Backsliders recovered. We find believers in many postures, and the society in several. We find formal and inward religion distinguished. We find the goodness of God, the pleasantness of religion, and the four last things, Death, Judgement, Heaven, and Hell, described. Wesley means business all the time. He is in deadly earnest. He has no leisure for frills and furbelows. He makes no concessions to human interests and the sentimental associations of religion. He condescends to write a morning hymn, it is true, and enriches the world by the glorious line, reminiscent of Dante, 'Christ, whose glory fills the skies', but Wesley forgets the time of day before he has written far.

Take a look at the work of Percy Dearmer, Vaughan Williams, and Martin Shaw as it is revealed in the Index to *Songs of Praise*. Here we find sixty hymns on the Christian Year and nearly as many on the Church and its ordinances;

but by far the greatest number of the titles are such as New Year, Spring, May, Morning, Noon, Evening, Hospitals, Social Service, Absent Friends. My account is unfair, because the bulk of the book is under the heading 'General', yet the contrast with Wesley remains valid and impressive. Dr. Dearmer and his friends do not arrange their hymns in the exclusively Christian and New Testament categories used by Wesley.

Do not suppose that I am merely praising Wesley and condemning Dearmer. As I distinguished Wesley from Watts, I now distinguish him from his successors. Watts sounded some notes which have been used to supplement Wesley; and more recent writers have supplemented him usefully too. But, when all is said, Wesley's obsession with the greatest things saved him, and us, from much that it is well to be saved from. Wesley's scheme did not tempt him to the vaguely religious poetizing which asks us to sing

> Day is dying in the west,

and chokes us with metaphorical confectionery. Nor does he indulge in those bird's-eye tours round the world which read like a versified *Holiday Haunts*:

> Sun and moon bright, night and moonlight,
>   Starry temples azure-floored;
> Cloud and rain, and wild wind's madness,
> Breeze that floats with genial gladness,
>   Praise ye, praise ye, God the Lord.
>
> Bond and freeman, land and sea man,
>   Earth with peoples widely stored,
> Wanderer lone o'er prairies ample,
> Full-voiced choir in costly temple,
>   Praise ye, praise ye, God the Lord!

Still farther is Wesley from the impieties of modern Roman and Anglo-Catholic hymns. These, like the degenerate late medieval and modern papal architecture, push aside the central acts of God in Christ in favour of the imaginary adventures of sinful mortals. When I glance at these hymn-books, they remind me of the beautiful blasphemy of the west front of Rheims Cathedral: there the Passion of the Son of God and His final Judgement of mankind serve as minor side ornaments to the central panel. And what is the central panel? The so-called Coronation of the Virgin, a matter with no place in history or theology or reputable legend. Precisely this blasphemy you will find in the hymn-books of certain schools, but you find it without the beauty of the Rheims blasphemy. God, as the Psalmist noted, has punished their own inventions. Not only orthodoxy, but the power of writing tolerable verse has deserted them.

Wesley's obsession was with the greatest things: I do not abandon my phrase, but I want to add to it. Despite my profound veneration of his verse, there are two or three things about Wesley's literary form that I regret—his use of compound adjectives like *soul-reviving*, and the unhappy use of *mine* and *every* in phrases like 'this heart of mine' and 'our every so and so'. It is the same with the content of the hymns. There is one feature which, to a Calvinist especially, seems unworthy of Wesley, though it is, to be sure, the defect of his qualities. Sometimes he speaks as if our feelings were of greater importance than I believe them to be. Occasionally a verse might give a hasty reader the impression that salvation almost depended on our feelings. It is perhaps the Pelagian shadow which has sometimes accompanied Arminianism, but it is an accidental and detachable shadow. For Wesley himself, the substance of revealed religion was too overwhelming to leave him at the mercy of his feelings, and it is but fair to Arminianism to remember that there were eighteenth-century Calvinists who suffered like Arminians from an over-emphasis on feelings about salvation. It was difficult for a man with Wesley's vivid experience not so to speak of experience as to make it take too prominent a place in the life of men who lacked the massive foundation of his instructed faith. Yet we may wish that by writing some hymns differently he had protected his ignorant and sensitive followers from the tortures of their ignorant sensitiveness.

I end by returning to my first inquiry. Why do Wesley's hymns confirm and restore our confidence, and build us up securely in our most holy faith? It is no doubt partly because they show us something of the life of one of the pure in heart who saw God. We may not see God. We cannot fail to see that Wesley saw Him. Purity of heart: we are near Wesley's secret there; scriptural holiness, purity of heart, inevitably reflected in his clear mind and limpid verse.

But I think I see another thing. Those very limitations which we have noticed in his hymn-book: his exclusion of all but God and Soul; his indifference to historical setting, cosmic backgrounds, times of day, seasons of the year; his frank neglect of any serious attempt to insert the gospel into natural religion, to tinge and colour normal human activities and occasions with a Christian hue; his ruthless inattention to everything that St. Thomas Aquinas wished to do to the natural order and the divine order—in all of this limitation we see one source of Wesley's power. Concern with all these things is no doubt needed in each generation; but the more appropriately and fully the work is done for a particular generation the more dated and transient it is. Wesley leaves all that aside. He is obsessed with the greatest things, and he confirms our faith because he shows us these above all the immediate, local, fashionable problems and objections to the faith. We move to the serener air. We sit in heavenly places with Christ Jesus; and simply to be taken there—that is, after all, the supreme confirmation of faith.

> What we have felt and seen
> With confidence we tell.

This same obsession with the greatest things lifts Wesley and us, his readers and singers, above all ecclesiastical divisions and discussions into the realm of religion. 'The Pleasantness of Religion', formal religion, inward religion, it is on these lines Wesley's thought moves, not on lines of valid and invalid, regular and irregular, historic and personal, priestly and prophetic ministrations. Wesley had his ecclesiastical opinions and could express them with his customary vigour and clarity; but, as he tells us himself, he escapes with joy from all such things to religion. The Bicentenary is indeed a recall to religion, to religion not merely when opposed to irreligion, but when opposed to religiousness, to theological gymnastics and ecclesiastical politics. I end with words which, for some reason, none of our editors will permit us to sing. You know them, but you shall hear them all again. In them Wesley tells you plainly what I have fumbled in my saying about that ampler air of pure religion: our security and our fellowship and our duty there:

CATHOLIC LOVE

Weary of all this wordy strife,
These notions, forms, and modes and names,
To Thee, the Way, the Truth, the Life,
Whose love my simple heart inflames,
Divinely taught at last I fly
With Thee and Thine to live and die.

Forth from the midst of Babel brought,
Parties and sects I cast behind;
Enlarged my heart, and free my thought
Where'er the latent truth I find;
The latent truth with joy to own
And bow to Jesus' name alone.

One with the little flock I rest,
The members sound who hold the Head,
The chosen few, with pardon blest,
And by the anointing spirit led.
Into the mind that was in Thee,
Into the depths of Deity.

My brethren, friends and kinsmen these
Who do my heavenly Father's will;
Who aim at perfect holiness,
And all Thy counsels to fulfil,
Athirst to be whate'er Thou art
And love their God with all their heart.

For these, howe'er in flesh disjoin'd,
Where'er dispersed o'er earth abroad,
Unfeigned unbounded love I find
And constant as the life of God;
Fountain of life, from thence it sprung,
As pure, as even, and as strong.

Joined to the hidden church unknown
In this sure bond of perfectness,
Obscurely safe, I dwell alone,
And glory in the uniting grace,
To me, to each believer given,
To all Thy saints in earth and heaven.

WESLEY'S HYMNS RECONSIDERED[1]

Samuel Taylor Coleridge, sometime Scholar of Jesus College in the University of Cambridge, once wrote some ingenious verses[2] to help his sons to remember the chief sorts of metre. If Coleridge had been a Methodist instead of a pilgrim from Anglicanism to Unitarianism and back again, he would have needed to do no such thing: he would have needed only to advise his boys to learn a selection of Wesley's hymns. From this point I begin. Leaving on one side for the moment any discussion of the meaning and content of the hymns, let us notice the metre, the rhyming, and the accentuation of them. These things deserve more attention than they usually get, and by this side road we shall approach the more important parts of the subject. By observing the mere form of the hymns, we shall learn more than we might expect.

Take the old hymn-book, *A Collection of Hymns for the Use of the People called Methodists. By the Rev. John Wesley, M.A., Sometime Fellow of Lincoln College, Oxford.* Get an edition with tunes, and turn to the index of metres. You will gasp with astonishment at the variety. You will be tempted to believe that Charles Wesley alone used as many metres in writing hymns as all other hymn-writers taken together. There are common metre, long metre, short metre, double short metre, 6.8s, 7s, 8s and 6s, 6s and 8s, 7s and 6s, 10s and 11s, 4.6s and 2.8s, 8s, 5s and 11s, 2.6s and 4.7s (to take a few examples) and the large number lumped together, very properly, as *peculiar metre.*

Wesley's variety is not fully represented by a mere enumeration of the syllables in each line, as that list might suggest. There is variety too in his arrangement of the stressed syllables. It is difficult to say much about this without coming under the

---

[1] A paper read before the Cambridge University Methodist Society on February 9, 1939.
[2] *Metrical Feet: Lesson for a Boy.*

condemnation passed by the Translators of the Authorized Version on a part of their own Preface to the Reader: 'We weary the unlearned, who need not know so much, and trouble the learned, who know it already.' Despite this, it is worth while to glance at a few technical matters in order to drive home what has been said about Wesley's infinite variety.

In English verse, the books tell us, the stressed and unstressed syllables take the place of the long and short syllables in classical Latin verse, and it is convenient to use some of the classical names for the metres. The metre most familiar to most of us is, I suppose, iambic: in this metre the line is divided into pairs of syllables with the stress falling on the second syllable.

> The way was long, the wind was cold.

This metre is familiar in the common metre of hymns:

> He breaks the power of cancelled sin,
> He sets the pris'ner free;

in long metre:

> Our Lord is risen from the dead;
> Our Jesus is gone up on high;

in short metre:

> To serve the present age,
> My calling to fulfil;

in 6.8s:

> O Thou eternal Victim, slain
> A sacrifice for guilty man;

in 8s and 6s:

O Love divine, how sweet Thou art:
When shall I find my willing heart
All taken up by Thee?

The exact opposite of the iambic metre is, of course, the trochaic. In this the stress falls on the first of the two syllables. Wesley is hardly less fond of this than of the iambic metre:

Jesu, Lover of my soul,
Let me to Thy bosom fly

Depth of mercy, can there be
Mercy still reserved for me?

Wesley sometimes combines the two, and so produces a very effective verse in 7s and 6s. A seven-syllable trochaic line is followed by a six-syllable iambic line:

Who is this gigantic foe
That proudly stalks along,
Overlooks the crowd below,
In brazen armour strong?

Notice the jumpy effect caused by the change in the alternate lines. It can be very moving; and it is a device peculiarly characteristic of Wesley. Here is another example:

Christ, whose glory fills the skies,

That famous Plant Thou art;

Tree of Life eternal, rise

In ev'ry longing heart!

Bid us find the food in Thee

For which our deathless spirits pine,

Fed with immortality,

And fill'd with love divine.

The quick succession of strong stresses in the last syllable of line 2 and in the first syllable of line 3 has the effect of knitting the verse very tight. The same device makes us rush almost breathlessly from line 4 to line 5. So it comes about that the four lines in the first half of the verse are not separated from the four lines in the second half, as would happen if either iambic or trochaic measures were used alone. The same structure is to be found in the famous hymn:

Son of God, if Thy free grace

Again hath raised me up,

Call'd me still to seek Thy face,

And giv'n me back my hope;

Still Thy timely help afford,

And all Thy loving kindness show:

Keep me, keep me, gracious Lord,

And never let me go!

So far all is simple, but have you considered what complications may lurk under that innocent-looking heading '8s'? It does not always mean a simple accumulation of iambic lines of eight syllables, as in 6.8s.

> Lo! God is here! let us adore,

or, as in long metre,

> Thy arm, Lord, is not shorten'd now.

Often it means something quite different. It covers a subtle system of accentuation, anapaestic, which Wesley uses for some of his most moving and most inspired hymns. No other hymn-writer, it is fairly safe to say, has approached him in mastery of this particular metre. In it we have no longer a simple alternation of stressed and unstressed syllables, but in the later part of each line we have two unstressed syllables followed by one stressed syllable. The line is not divided in the way that we have already observed, 2 : 2 : 2 : 2, but 2 : 3 : 3. The supreme example of this is to be seen in what is perhaps the most passionate and exalted of all Wesley's hymns:

> Thou Shepherd of Israel, and mine,
>
> The joy and desire of my heart,
>
> For closer communion I pine,
>
> I long to reside where Thou art.
>
> The pasture I languish to find,
>
> Where all who their Shepherd obey
>
> Are fed, on Thy bosom reclined,
>
> And screen'd from the heat of the day.

We have a yet more complicated arrangement of anapaestic measures in hymns like:

> .   / . . /
> Come, let us anew
>
> . / .   . /
> Our journey pursue,
>
> .   /   .   . /
> Roll round with the year,
>
> / . . / . . / . . /
> And never stand still till the Master appear.

This is an amazing, magical metre which Wesley used with the surest touch. Hardly any one else, I think, has succeeded in it, or even tried to master it. The accumulation of anapaests in the last line is most subtle.

Nothing shows Wesley's superb mastery of metre more than his use of the perverse, unnatural, and almost ludicrous metre 2.6s and 4.7s. On this tight rope, to all appearance fit only for acrobatics, Wesley moves with ease and confidence and grace. In this metre, indeed, he writes some of his most characteristic hymns. The metre 2.6s and 4.7s is so artificial as to be at first, even in Wesley's hands, slightly irritating and precious; but once you have made yourself familiar with it (especially if you have taken the trouble to see precisely what Wesley is doing) it holds you.

> /   /   /
> How weak the thoughts, and vain,
>
> /   /   /
> Of self-deluding men;
>
> /   /   /   /
> Men, who, fix'd to earth alone,
>
> /   /   /   /
> Think their houses shall endure,
>
> /   /   /   /
> Fondly call their lands their own,
>
> /   /   /   /
> To their distant heirs secure.

Fairly flat that seems: an uninspired, almost solicitor-like version of a not very attractive psalm. Yes, but wait till Wesley has left the solicitor's office. By the time he has reached verse 4 he is finding his wings:

> High on Immanuel's land
> We see the fabric stand;
> From a tott'ring world remove
> To our steadfast mansion there:
> Our inheritance above
> Cannot pass from heir to heir.
>
> Those amaranthine bowers
> (Unalienably ours)
> Bloom, our infinite reward,
> Rise, our permanent abode;
> From the founded world prepared;
> Purchased by the blood of God.

Unless you have in mind the precise wording of Psalm xlix; unless you catch the reference to the fourteenth chapter of St. John in *mansion;* unless you lick your lips over the contrast between the Saxon language of the earlier verses and the gathering Latinisms as the hymn proceeds: *mansion, inheritance, amaranthine, unalienably, infinite, permanent;* unless you relish the pure Latin construction *from the founded world;* unless you catch the deftly sudden change in the position of one stress in

> High on Immanuel's land;

you do not begin to learn the art of Wesley or to understand why he dominates the lesser fry as he does.

Examine another hymn, also about heaven, in the same perverse metre. It is clear that, like every other man who knows that he has the power of doing something difficult, Wesley enjoys exercising his skill. He bends the intractable material to his purpose with a certain zest.

> Again we lift our voice,
>
> And shout our solemn joys;
>
> Cause of highest raptures this,
>
> Raptures that shall never fail;
>
> See a soul escaped to bliss,
>
> Keep the Christian Festival.
>
> Our friend is gone before
>
> To that celestial shore;
>
> He hath left his mates behind,
>
> He hath all the storms outrode,
>
> Found the rest we toil to find
>
> Landed in the arms of God.

Regard for space prevents the transcription of the rest of this hymn, notable for its dignity and its superb faith. We observe in passing the reminiscence of the familiar lines of Spenser about rest after toil and the natural way in which it is combined with the reminiscence of the text in Deuteronomy xxxiii. 27.

The verse known as 10s and 11s presents another very subtle combination. For some reason the insertion of an insignificant, odd, extra syllable in the last two lines gives the verse a lilt that four symmetrical lines of ten syllables each has not got. The verse is anapaestic. The first half of all four lines is the same. In the first couplet the second half line merely repeats the first half line; but in the second couplet we come on the extra syllables which give the leaping effect.

> O what shall we do Our Saviour to love?
>
> To make us anew, Come, Lord, from above!
>
> The fruit of Thy passion, Thy holiness give:
>
> Give us the salvation Of all that believe.

It is not until we have explored a few of his metrical mazes that we begin to understand why in his thousands of lines Wesley so rarely lets the accent fall on the wrong syllable. Only a master of versification could trip so seldom, but, of course, unless he had been a master of versification Wesley could never have written anything whatsoever in many of these metres. When you take into consideration the large flank which Wesley presents for attack, it is astonishing how few successful attacks can be made on him. Most hymn-writers with only a tenth of the number of hymns in our books give us a larger number of unhappily placed stresses. Wesley rarely offends by writing such a line as that which is a sad blemish in Crossman's one well-known hymn, 'My song is love unknown'. Crossman lets the stress fall intolerably in one solemn line:

> They rise and needs will have
>
> My *dear* Lord made away.

The careless reader may think that he has caught Wesley napping sometimes, and at times, of course, Wesley does nod disastrously; but before the amateur critic like myself boasts too rashly about catching Wesley out, he should study Dr. Bett's invaluable book on the Wesley poetry. [1] There, with the modesty of high scholarship, Dr. Bett traces the changes in the pronunciation of certain words such as *confessor* and *acceptable* which have made some of Wesley's verses seem (to the ignorant) incorrectly stressed.

More than most writers, Wesley makes the end of his lines correspond with natural pauses in his thought. The sound and the sense coincide. This is it which makes his verse specially suitable for singing. This is it which makes it possible to sing his hymns so easily to the so-called 'old-fashioned' tunes, the florid, repetitious tunes, in which any line may be repeated almost at random in almost accidental combinations. But even Wesley's arrangement of lines does not always win applause. At times the meaning 'runs over' the end of one line into the middle of the next:

> Ah, soften, melt this rock, and may
> Thy blood wash all these stains away!

and

> Relieve the thirsty soul, the faint
> Revive, illuminate the blind.

This seems ugly when it is contrasted with the next couplet, written in the more usual happy style:

> The mournful cheer, the drooping lead,
> And heal the sick, and raise the dead.

But before we say, or even think, too much about these 'irregular' lines, we should ponder what Dr. Bett has to say about them and the light that they may throw on the tangled problem of separating the compositions of John from those of Charles.

One part of the attractiveness of the older hymn-writers is their frequent use of proper names. They inherited this habit

---

[1] *The Hymns of Methodism in their Literary Relations*, Epworth Press.

from their predecessors, who had simply paraphrased Holy
Scripture. Paraphrasers, it is clear, had no choice. They had to
take the rough with the smooth. They had to boil down the
weirdest geographical and personal names into rigid metre.
Dexterity in the art, once acquired, persisted; and it was
bequeathed to hymn-writers.

It is by no means only in his paraphrases that Wesley uses
proper names. He knew what our psychologists are now
giving one another Ph.D.s for discovering by research in dark
rooms with coloured slips of paper. He knew that the use of a
proper name with associations may start or clinch a train of
thought more effectively than a flood of colourless words will
start or clinch it. To you and to me, with our beggarly knowledge of Holy Scripture, this magic is less potent than it was to
Wesley. What was once moving may seem to us only quaint.
Even you and I, it is true, can pick up a reference to the Church
as Sion or Jerusalem, a reference to death as Jordan, a reference
to heaven as Canaan. But how much farther can we go? What
does a modern congregation make of

> None is like Jeshurun's God?

We may not have got to the pass of the undergraduate who
politely enquired, 'Yes, but who *was* Jehovah?' but, if we
are honest, many of us might ask, 'Who was Jeshurun?' In the
hymn beginning

> O Great Mountain, who art thou,
> Immense, immovable?

how many will catch the reference in the line

> My Zerubbabel is near?

More easy are the allusions in the following:

> In soft Laodicean ease
> We sleep our useless lives away

and

> Less grievous will the judgment-day
> To Sodom and Gomorrah prove.

and (as we used to be allowed to sing in 'O for a thousand tongues')

> Cast all your sins into the deep,
> And wash the Aethiop white.

But this is more difficult:

> Take when Thou wilt into Thy hands,
> And as Thou wilt require;
> Resume by the Chaldean bands,
> Or the devouring fire.

The first and the second Adam are never far from Wesley's thought, and no hymn-writer has more happily used the Pauline antithesis. One mention of the name must be made, for it gives a classic summary of St. Paul's teaching concerning the solidarity of lost and of saved mankind:

> Adam, descended from above!
> Federal Head of all mankind.

From such a use of Holy Scripture it is but a short step to the paraphrase proper. Wesley's paraphrases have a distinctive quality of their own. Most men's paraphrases tend to be wooden in their exactness. They often say in feebler language what has been said superbly in Holy Scripture; and the better we remember the scriptural words the worse we think of the paraphrase. Wesley avoids this peril by the freedom with which he paraphrases. He is very bold. His verses are a commentary on the passage as well as a restatement of it. Nowhere has he more profited from the example of his master, Dr. Watts. Dr. Watts provided evangelical interpretations for psalms and for Old Testament passages and Wesley uses the same method, but with even greater boldness.

Wesley's paraphrases form but a small part of the book, but among them are some of his masterpieces. They deserve more exact study than they have received. How are we to select? There is the sublime treatment of the Song of Moses in Deuteronomy xxxiii: 'None is like Jeshurun's God.' There is the promise of the Corner Stone in Zechariah iv: 'O Great Mountain, who art thou?' There is the survey of the Promised Land from Pisgah—ravishing stuff indeed:

> O that I might at once go up!
> No more on this side Jordan stop,
>   But now the land possess;
> This moment end my legal years;
> Sorrows, and sins, and doubts, and fears,
>   A howling wilderness.

There is the thirty-fifth chapter of Isaiah: 'The wilderness and the solitary place.' Here we note the use of proper names:

> Lo! abundantly they bloom;
> Lebanon is hither come;
> Carmel's stores the heavens dispense,
> Sharon's fertile excellence.

The Revised Version (in the interest of zoological truth, no doubt) degrades the dragons of this chapter into mere jackals: 'in the habitation of *jackals* where they lay.' Wesley, with more inspired imagination, increases the vigour of the Authorized Version not by merely retaining the dragons, but by bestowing old age upon them, and so making them the type of Satan, the old Dragon.

> Where the ancient Dragon lay,
> Open for Thyself a way!
> There let holy tempers rise,
> All the fruits of Paradise.

A last example of Wesley's paraphrases is provided by the confused and magical mystery of the Christmas lesson in Isaiah ix. Of the Authorized Version of that chapter, Sir Arthur Quiller-Couch has said: 'the old translators made nonsense, and, in two passages at least, stark nonsense.' The Revised Version straightens out the meaning into somewhat prosaic common sense. Wesley solved the problem in a third way. *'For every battle of the warrior is with confused noise, and garments rolled in blood; but this shall be with burning and fuel of fire.'* 'Granted the rhythmical antithesis,' writes Sir Arthur Quiller-Couch, 'where is the real antithesis, the difference, the improvement? If a battle there must be, how is burning better than garments rolled in blood? and, in fine, what is it all about?' The inquiry is answered in the Revised Version, as Sir Arthur Quiller-Couch points out, and every wise lover of the English Bible will have Sir Arthur's words by heart.[1] Yet it is still worth while seeing what Wesley makes of the matter. Here is his paraphrase and his notion of the reality of the antithesis:

> Thou hast our bonds in sunder broke,
>   Took all our load of guilt away;
> From sin, the world, and Satan's yoke,
>   (Like Israel saved in Midian's day,)
> Redeem'd us by our conquering Lord,
> Our Gideon, and His Spirit's sword.
>
> Not like the warring sons of men,
>   With shout, and garments roll'd in blood,
> Our Captain doth the fight maintain;
>   But lo! the burning Spirit of God
> Kindles in each a secret fire,
> And all our sins as smoke expire!

Wesley's hymns provide, as we have seen, an education in the use of proper names; but he deals not only with proper names.

[1] *On the Art of Writing*, lectures VI and VII; *On the Art of Reading*, lectures VIII, IX, and X.

To sing or to read his hymns is to expand one's vocabulary and to learn the power of pregnant words. In general, Wesley prefers the Saxon word, but no one can more effectively use Latin words either alone or in combination. Here are a few typical lines:

> Here we in the spirit breathe
> The quintessence of praise.
>
> .   .   .   .   .
>
> Joyful consentaneous sound,
> Sweetest symphony of praise.

That couplet, Latin and Greek, ends one verse; the next ends with pure Saxon:

> Only sing and praise and love.

Here is another fine set of strong words:

> Implunged in the crystal abyss,
> And lost in the ocean of God.

And here is a full mixture of Latin and Saxon, with powerful repetitions:

> Thee let me drink, and thirst no more
> For drops of finite happiness;
> Spring up, O Well, in heavenly power
> In streams of pure, perennial peace,
> In joy, that none can take away,
> In life, which shall for ever stay.

Wesley does not stop at words derived from Latin and Greek. In one famous passion hymn, which Dr. Bett has fully discussed, he goes farther and refers to a classical legend in severely classical language: 'Great Pan is dead.'

> Lo! the powers of heaven He shakes;
> Nature in convulsions lies;
> Earth's profoundest centre quakes;
> The great Jehovah dies!

> Dies the glorious cause of all,
> The true eternal *Pan*
> Falls to raise us from our fall,
> To ransom sinful man!
> Well may *Sol* withdraw his light. . . .

We may compare the reference to Thor and Woden:

> Less guilty if with those of old
> We worshipped *Thor* and *Woden* still.

As we should expect in the hymns of an eighteenth-century writer, there are in Wesley's some words and phrases that sound oddly to-day. His rhymes betray a few changes in pronunciation. He rhymes words like *join* and *mine*, as every one must have noticed. When a word has changed in meaning, it has usually changed for the worse. Words like *bloody* and *blasted* are to-day less solemn and impressive than they once were; but in the main the changes are fewer than we might have expected. The impression made by Wesley's language is very different from that made by Watts's. Watts was born only one generation before Wesley. He was thirty-four years older, but he speaks what is almost a different language. You cannot read many lines of Watts without coming on some grotesque or quaint expression. Watts used many words in a fashion quite unlike our own. That is why it is so difficult to use most of Watts's hymns to-day. His book, crammed as it is with magnificent things, has a decidedly antiquarian aroma. Wesley's usage is separated from ours by a less gulf. Only occasionally does he write an odd line like this on death:

> And when the storms of life shall cease,
> Jesus, in that important hour,
> In death as life be Thou my guide;

or this:

> But, O almighty God of love,
> Into Thy hands the matter take.

No one understood better than Wesley what may be called the conventional literary devices. Elsewhere I have written at some length about his use of the chiasmus, of which he was an accomplished master.

> We now Thy promised presence claim,
>   Sent to disciple all mankind,
> Sent to baptize into Thy name,
>   We now Thy promised presence find.

On the simple device of repetition he rings endless changes. A whole essay would be needed even to begin to do them justice. One hymn alone will provide several examples.

There is, first, the simple repetition of the invocation:

> Come, Holy Ghost, all-quick'ning fire,
>   Come, and in me delight to rest;

then with an echo of it, we continue:

> Drawn by the lure of strong desire,
>   O *come* and consecrate my breast!

In the next verse we begin again with the simple repetition:

> If now Thy influence I feel,
>   If now in Thee begin to live,

and we continue with a variant of the same device:

> Still to my heart Thyself reveal;
>   *Give* me Thyself, for ever *give*.

Next comes, not repetition, but a pair of parallel phrases:

> A point my good, a drop my store,

and now the last line of this verse and the first line of the next
verse are tied together by a treble repetition: a repetition of
these three words: *eager, ask, pant.*

> A point my good, a drop my store,
> Eager I ask, I pant for more.

> Eager for Thee I ask and pant;
> So strong the principle divine,

and so on.

Contrast the effect of verses so knit and so coloured with (let
us say) the verses of that casual Papist rhymer Faber. Faber adds
line to line, careful of nothing, if the second line comes near to
rhyming with the fourth. He not only does not achieve anything
more: he does not even attempt anything more. Here is the
wretched stuff; but we ought not to call it careless or casual, for
we must observe the care with which he has packed it with false
stresses:

> O it is hard to work for God,
>   To rise and take His part
> Upon this battle-field of earth,
>   And not sometimes lose heart.

It would make first-rate prose.

> He hides Himself so wondrously
>   As if there were no God,
> He is least seen when all the powers
>   Of ill are most abroad.

Yet our hardest words must not be for Faber, but for the
Methodist editors alike in 1904 and in 1933. Wesley had
built his hymn on the principle of repetition, the climax being
in the two adjacent verses (as we have seen). One ended

> Eager I ask, I pant for more.

The other began

> Eager for Thee I ask and pant.

Now, unless the thing had happened, we could not have believed it. The 1904 editors printed the earlier verse without the later; the 1933 editors printed the later verse without the earlier. They agreed only in this: that what Wesley had joined together his followers should put asunder. One is tempted to inquire if any one in 1904 or in 1933 had taken the trouble to read through the whole hymn.

A more cumulative effect of repetition we get in 'Holy Lamb, who Thee confess'; but note, first, the perfect balance of the first four lines.

> Early in the temple met,
> Let us still our Saviour greet;
> Nightly to the mount repair,
> Join our praying Pattern there.
> There . . .

Notice this repetition linking the two halves of the verse and preparing us for the crashing repetitions to follow:

> There by wrestling faith obtain
> Power to work for God again;
> Power His image to retrieve,
> Power, like Thee, our Lord, to live.

By a similar device in

> Come, Thou long-expected Jesus,
>   Born to set Thy people free,

we have the word *born* appearing early in the verse to prepare us for the triple use that is to follow:

> Born Thy people to deliver,
>   Born a child and yet a king,
> Born to reign in us for ever;
>   Now Thy gracious kingdom bring.

Still more daring, but completely triumphant, is the sixfold repetition of *one* in this hymn on the Communion of Saints:

> Build us in one body up,
> Call'd in one high calling's hope;
> One the Spirit Whom we claim;
> One the pure baptismal flame;
> One the faith, and common Lord,
> One the Father lives adored,
> Over, through, and in us all
> God incomprehensible.

And yet (is it possible?) when we want a hymn about our unity, we have the effrontery to forget Wesley and to sing Baring-Gould's ditty:

> Through the night of doubt and sorrow.

Wesley's art does not exhaust itself in the choice and use of single words. His hymns have a quality which is perhaps fairly described as dramatic and architectural. In a few lines Wesley sketches a background. At once you are made aware of a vista, a setting, and an atmosphere. You see and feel and hear and even smell the action as it proceeds. Often it is liturgical action. It is shown, perhaps, supremely in 'Victim Divine, Thy grace we claim' (but not in the fragment printed in the new *Methodist Hymn-book*) and in 'Entered the holy place above'. This art Wesley learnt, we cannot doubt, from the Apocalypse. Take this exalted passage on the Beatific Vision from 'Come on, my partners in distress':

> That great mysterious Deity
> We soon with open face shall see;
>   The beatific sight
> Shall fill heaven's sounding courts with praise,
> And wide diffuse the golden blaze
>   Of everlasting light.

> The Father shining on His throne,
> The glorious ſo-eternal Son,
>   The Spirit, one and seven,
> Conspire our rapture to complete;
> And lo! we fall before His feet,
>   And silence heightens heaven.

Wesley has added *heightens* to what he found in the Apocalypse about silence in Heaven. It is one of the sharp strokes which illustrates the soundness and the brilliance of his intuition.

If we are to measure the merit of Wesley here we must set his picture beside that of, say, Kelly. Kelly shared much of Wesley's faith and experience. He is always trying to say the same things. He is sincere and he is likeable. But his achievement is not equal to his good intention. In trying to be sublime, he is so vigorous as to be almost irreverent; and yet, for all his loud emphasis, we feel that when he comes to great things he is sadly guilty of under-statement. He is like the schoolgirl who wrote of the Apostle, 'St. Luke was a good man'. It was true, but it was so inadequate as to be patronizing.

Contrast Kelly's picture of the final glory of Heaven with Wesley's. Kelly wrote:

> Hark! those bursts of acclamation!
>   Hark! those loud triumphant chords!
> Jesus takes the highest station;
>   O what joy the sight affords!

The last line is exquisite bathos, and the last couplet suggests a certain relief in finding that the issue has not, after all, been different.

Contrast again Bridges' lines:

> All hail! Redeemer, hail!
>   (For Thou hast died for me)
> Thy praise shall never, never fail
>   Throughout eternity.

In an attempt to be personal, the author pushes himself forward in the wrong way. It is an unfortunate version of the song of the redeemed in the Apocalypse. Moreover, *never, never fail* is an example of precisely the wrong way to repeat a word. It is like Watts's unhappy line

> There shall we see His face,
> And never, never sin.

We more than half fear that the word is repeated, not for emphasis, but only to fill up the required number of syllables. Set beside such lines the moving repetitions which we have studied in Wesley. Nothing is weaker than repetition weakly done. Nothing is stronger than repetition strongly done. In Wesley's jubilation we discern the dignity and the reverence due to the Son of God. The personal note is not missing, but it is subordinate; and there is no half-suggestion that the event might have been otherwise.

> Jesus the Saviour reigns,
>   The God of truth and love;
> When He had purged our stains,
>   He took His seat above:
> Lift up your heart, lift up your voice;
> Rejoice; again I say, rejoice.

That exhortation is more vigorous and more scriptural than Kelly's exclamation:

> O what joy the sight affords!

To conclude this matter, there is Wesley's less familiar verse in which all the notes are struck:

> Extol His kingly power;
>   Kiss the exalted Son,
> Who died, and lives, to die no more,
>   High on His Father's throne.
> Our Advocate with God,
>   He undertakes our cause,
> And spreads through all the earth abroad
>   The victory of His cross.

It is time to leave these smaller matters of language and to say something of the more general character of Wesley's hymns. The first quality which must strike us is their faithful, moving, but utterly unsentimental record of every phase of religious feeling. There is no mood of the Christian soul that is not reflected in Wesley's hymns. If you are depressed, elated, energetic, enervated, full of doubt, secure in faith, you can find in Wesley's hymns, as you can find nowhere else but in the Psalms, the appropriate words in which to pour out your soul to God. You can indeed often find in Wesley's hymns words more appropriate than you will find in the Psalms, because Wesley's are Christian words. They are written for you against the background of the Cross. They do not need the interpretation and the allegorizing which the Psalmist's words sometimes need and which we are sometimes too badly broken to give. Here is one example. Can we hope to express repentance better than this?

> Stay, Thou insulted Spirit, stay,
>   Though I have done Thee such despite,
> Nor cast the sinner quite away,
>   Nor take Thine everlasting flight.
>
> Though I have steel'd my stubborn heart,
>   And still shook off my guilty fears;
> And vex'd, and urged Thee to depart,
>   For many long rebellious years:
>
> Though I have most unfaithful been,
>   Of all who e'er Thy grace received;
> Ten thousand times Thy goodness seen,
>   Ten thousand times Thy goodness grieved:
>
> Yet O! the chief of sinners spare,
>   In honour of my great High-Priest;
> Nor in Thy righteous anger swear
>   To exclude me from Thy people's rest.

> This only woe I deprecate;
>   This only plague I pray remove;
> Nor leave me in my lost estate;
>   Nor curse me with this want of love.

But, though Wesley portrays all feelings potently, there is *one* note in his hymns which rings out clear above all the rest. It is the note of confidence, heavenly and inviolable confidence: *The best of all is, God is with us.*

> As far from danger as from fear,
>   While love, almighty love, is near.
> What mighty troubles hast Thou shewn
>   Thy feeble, tempted followers here!
> We have through fire and water gone,
>   But saw Thee on the floods appear,
> But felt Thee present in the flame,
> And shouted our Deliverer's name.

(In passing, we note the characteristic interpretation of the Psalmist's words, 'we went through fire and through water,' by references to our Lord walking on the Sea of Galilee and to the appearance of One like the Son of God in the Babylonian furnace.)

> Lord, we Thy will obey,
>   And in Thy pleasure rest;
> We, only we, can say,
>   'Whatever is, is best'.
> Faith, mighty faith, the promise sees,
>   And looks to that alone;
> Laughs at impossibilities,
>   And cries, 'It shall be done!'

(In passing, we note another favourite device of Wesley's: he likes to use a word which refers us to a passage of Holy Scripture, but to change and often to strengthen its meaning. Faith 'laughs' at impossibilities. Wesley has taken the notion of laughing from the story of Sarah's incredulity about Isaac's birth. Originally it was Sarah who laughed in scornful unbelief. Wesley baptizes Sarah's laughter, and in his scheme of things it is faith, not unfaith, which laughs. The point is small, but very characteristic. We catch, too, in line four a reference to Pope's dictum, *Whatever is, is right*. Stated by Pope as a general truth, it is open to question. Wesley rewrites it in the light of Romans viii. 28. He makes it less general, and so, though more emphatic, less questionable.)

Why this confidence? What is its basis? We need look no farther than the hymns themselves. Wesley's confidence is rooted in the orthodox, catholic, evangelical faith. Nowhere have you a better body of sound doctrine. If you know Wesley's hymns, you receive (whether you wish it or not) a magnificent course of instruction in high dogmatic theology. Here is a prayer to the Holy Ghost:

> Thy witness with my spirit bear,
> That God, my God, inhabits there,
>   Thou, with the Father and the Son,
> Eternal light's co-eval beam:—
> Be Christ in me, and I in Him,
>   Till perfect we are made in one.

Here is an address to the Son:

> Effulgence of the Light Divine,
> Ere rolling planets knew to shine,
>   Ere time its ceaseless course began;
> Thou, when the appointed hour was come,
> Didst not abhor the virgin's womb,
>   But, God with God, wast man with man.

Here is a sacramental prayer to the Father (copied, I suspect, by Dr. Bright in his better-known, but less excellent, hymn, 'And now, O Father, mindful of the love'):

> With solemn faith we offer up,
>   And spread before Thy glorious eyes,
> That only ground of all our hope,
>   That precious, bleeding Sacrifice,
> Which brings Thy grace on sinners down,
> And perfects all our souls in one.

Nothing is more untrue than to represent the heart of Wesley's religion as personal experience or even personal feeling. The heart of Wesley's religion is sound doctrine. The common misrepresentation of him can be cherished only by those who never read, for instance, the eucharistic hymn which begins:

> And shall I let Him go?
>   If now I do not feel
> The streams of Living Water flow,
>   Shall I forsake the Well?
>   .   .   .   .   .
> Because He saith, Do this,
>   This I will always do.

We find in Wesley, then, not merely the comfort and the drive of personal religion, not merely a heart strangely warmed and hands vigorous for the fight: we find displayed in the hymns the secret power that warms the heart and teaches the fingers to fight. To-day many of us envy Wesley's enthusiasm and Wesley's assault upon the world. We do well to envy; and we can perceive in the hymns that what we envy is the product of something else. The hymns present to us, time and again, glorious confessions of faith in the Incarnate Word of God, confessions in which Wesley has rarely been equalled and never surpassed. Very God and Very Man: it is that vision which inspires and drives Wesley, as it inspired and drove the writers of the New Testament.

> Fairer than all the earth-born race,
>   Perfect in comeliness Thou art;
> Replenish'd are Thy lips with grace,
>   And full of love Thy tender heart:
> God ever blest! we bow the knee,
> And own all fulness dwells in Thee.

The greatness of Wesley's hymns lies in the exactness with which they recapture and represent the life of the New Testament. In them, as in it, we move high above all ecclesiastical divisions and out of hearing of almost all theological controversies. Wesley speaks the language of the Gospels and the Epistles. The dramatic action of his hymns is drawn from the Apocalypse. His picture of a Christian society is copied from the Acts of the Apostles. We see all this in the great Easter hymn as savagely and as criminally truncated in the new *Methodist Hymn-book* as it was even in the *English Hymnal.* Here are the verses which no one now permits us to sing: verses in which Wesley's theology, literary art, use of Old Testament allegory, and dominant confidence all find illustration:

> What though once we perish'd all,
> Partners in our parents' fall?
> Second life we all receive;
> In our heavenly Adam live.

> Risen with Him we upward move,
> Still we seek the things above;
> Still pursue and kiss the Son,
> Seated on His Father's throne.

> Scarce a thought on earth bestow,
> Dead to all we leave below;
> Heav'n our aim and loved abode,
> Hid our life with Christ in God.

> Hid, till Christ our life appear,
> Glorious in His members here,
> Join'd to Him we then shall shine,
> All immortal, all divine.

That is the faith; but is it without works and dead?

That bloody banner see,
  And, in your Captain's sight,
Fight the good fight of faith with me,
  My fellow-soldiers, fight!
In mighty phalanx join'd,
  To battle all proceed;
Arm'd with the unconquerable mind
  Which was in Christ your Head.

The world cannot withstand
  Its ancient Conqueror;
The world must sink beneath the hand
  Which arms us for the war.
This is our victory!
  Before our faith they fall;
Jesus hath died for you and me;
  Believe, and conquer all.

THE HYMNS OF DR. ISAAC WATTS [1]

Dr. HENRY BETT and Dr. Albert Peel have recently revived the respectable game of comparing the hymns of Watts and the hymns of Wesley. I shall have to take a turn or two at it myself before I finish this paper. Indeed, no one can read Watts without having Wesley in mind, and nothing will enable a man to see the greatness of Watts's hymns so well as a thorough knowledge of Wesley's. I make no apology, then, for beginning and continuing and ending with the comparison at the back of my mind. Watts himself began the game when he said with the generosity of a Congregationalist and the exaggeration of a preacher that Wesley's 'Wrestling Jacob' was worth all that he himself had ever written.

This paper is about Dr. Watts's hymns, not about Dr. Watts. We must, for all that, take a look at Dr. Watts himself. He was born in 1674 and died at the age of seventy-four in 1748. His life, that is to say, covered the period in which Protestant Dissent won its permanent place in English society. When Watts was born, Protestant Dissent was proscribed and persecuted. When he was a boy, there occurred the decisive struggle with Popery and the Popish King, James II. The Glorious Revolution of 1688 brought security to the Church of England and Toleration to Protestant Dissenters. When Watts was in middle life the end of the Stuarts and the accession of the House of Hanover marked the failure of the Tory attack on the settlement of 1688, an attack aimed especially at the Dissenters, but promising a revival of Popery too. At the very end of his life, Dr. Watts had the satisfaction of witnessing in the failure of the '45 the collapse of the Young Pretender, and the final deliverance of Great Britain from the dangers that had menaced it since the death of Oliver Cromwell. The Constitution was saved

---

[1] A paper read to the University Congregational Society in Cambridge on Sunday, October 17, 1937.

from Divine Right. Protestantism was saved from France and the Pope. Dissent was saved from Toryism and persecution. Watts, then, was one of those fortunate persons whose life co-incides with the increasing triumph of his own cause. The right people win. The wicked are cast down. All things—visibly—work together for good to them that love God. The note of cheerfulness—perhaps the most distinct note in Watts's poetry —comes appropriately from such a setting.

That is the setting. We glance now at the career. Watts's grandfather was a naval officer who served under Blake, the Cromwellian admiral, one of our greatest naval heroes. Watts's father, as became a Dissenter after the collapse of the Rule of the Saints, led a humbler life. He was in business in Southampton. But remember the grandfather and observe Watts's rather war-like patriotism, his pride in the 'sceptred isle', 'set in the silver sea', in the Navy which protects it, in the naval traditions of our race. All this, which comes leaking through Watts's pious prayers for Britain, reminds us of Blake's lieutenant. Watts himself was two things: a minister and a scholar, great in each work. His studies ruined his health. In 1712, just before he was forty, he went to live with Sir Thomas Abney, of Abney Park, and he spent the rest of his life there. He did not com-pletely abandon the active ministry, however, and at the time of his death he was something like a national figure. He has a memorial in Westminster Abbey. About his scholarship we observe that, vast as it was, he amassed it under the difficulties which hampered all Dissenters till 1870. He was excluded from Oxford and Cambridge, and went to a Dissenting academy. The academies tried to do what the national universities refused to do for Dissenters. Compared with Oxford and Cambridge, the academies had many disadvantages, but they had one notable advantage. On them the dead hand of mathematics and classics lay less heavily. They developed a wider notion of education. Philosophy, natural science, history, modern languages found a place. Accordingly, Dr. Watts possessed an encyclopaedic sort of scholarship, less fine and nice, it might be, in the classics than the most polished Oxford man of his time might have, but vastly wider in scope and more liberal in tendency. I do not mean that Dr. Watts knew little Greek and Latin. He was accomplished in both; but he knew other things too.

So much, but no more, does it seem necessary to say by way of introducing the author. We now open the book: *The Psalms of David imitated in New Testament Language together with Hymns and Spiritual Songs.* It has two parts, as the title indicates, and they are of about equal length. In the first part Dr. Watts presents a metrical version of the Book of Psalms. It is not a mere reproduction of the 150 psalms. Some are omitted. Some are abbreviated. Some are represented by more than one version in different metres. Some are divided into several parts. All are baptized into the Christian faith. But Watts shall tell you in his own words what he has done:

> 'It is necessary to divest *David* and *Asaph,* &c. of every other Character but that of a *Psalmist* and a *Saint,* and to *make them always speak the common Sense of a Christian.* . . . Where the Psalmist describes Religion by the *Fear* of God, I have often joined *Faith and Love* to it: . . . Where he talks of sacrificing *Goats or Bullocks,* I rather chuse to mention the Sacrifice of *Christ, the Lamb of God*: Where he attends the *Ark with Shouting* in *Zion,* I sing the *Ascension of my Saviour* into Heaven, or his *Presence in his Church* on Earth.'

The second part of the book contains hymns. First comes a book of hymns 'collected from the Holy Scriptures'—that is to say, paraphrases of both Old and New Testament passages. Second is a book of hymns 'composed on Divine Subjects'— that is to say, hymns as we should understand the word, freely composed without particular reference to Holy Scripture. Third, and last, are hymns 'prepared for the holy ordinance of the Lord's Supper'. As Watts had ended his Psalter by six versions of *Gloria Patri* in various metres, so he ends the hymn-book by others. Some are in the form of hymns. Some are single verses. To these he adds four hosannas to the Son of God. The result is a very substantial volume.

I shall not pretend to any bibliographical knowledge of Watts's works. If you want that knowledge, you will find it in Julian's *Dictionary of Hymnology*. I mention only that the *Hymns* were published in 1707 and enlarged in a second edition in 1709; and that ten years later the *Psalms* were published. We will take the volume as it stands compacted of these two.

Nor shall I give you, what I am indeed unfit to give you, an historical sketch of hymn-singing in our churches. I note only that Watts is a pioneer. Hymns were being sung in our churches in the late seventeenth century; but there was a prejudice against them as both Popish and unscriptural. That prejudice died hard; and, what was worse, the supply of English hymns was meagre and poor. To Watts more than to any other man is due the triumph of the hymn in English worship. All later hymn-writers, even when they excel him, are his debtors; and it is possible to hold that his work for hymns is greater than Charles Wesley's, even if as a writer of hymns we place him a little lower than Wesley. Metrical psalms in great numbers there were before Watts, and they were much used. But here, as in his hymns, Watts was a pioneer. In his Christian interpretation of the Psalms, he had predecessors, but no one had so thoroughly carried out the plan before.

In examining what Dr. Watts wrote, we must then always remember that he is hewing his way through an almost unexplored territory, and that his successors, not having his rough work to do again, will be able to polish and improve. We must expect him to make many experiments that fail, and to try many arrangements before he finds the best. His book is a laboratory of experiments. Only in a few places can we expect him to bring one off. Another set of conditions hampered him. He was writing for congregations that were often ignorant. His hymns had to be suitable to be announced and sung line by line by illiterates. He had to write in only a few well-known metres, a limitation of which he often complained.

I claim at this point the historian's privilege: the privilege of mentioning dates. The hymns were published in 1707. Watts's mind, that is to say, was formed in the seventeenth century. He is a seventeenth- rather than an eighteenth-century writer. This appears in that quality of his verse which friends call quaint, and enemies grotesque. When Watts's taste was set the English language had not undergone that purging and purifying, that rationalizing and simplification, which we associate with the name of Addison. Here we find a contrast between Watts and Wesley. Watts's forebears wrote crabbed, allusive, tortuous prose and verse. Charles Wesley's forebears wrote the slick and polished stuff. To write great theology in common metre, long metre, or in 6.8s is not easy even if you have a perfect command of metre; but Watts found no metre ready tamed for his use. Read the metrical psalter of the Church of Scotland, and you will get a picture of the untamed, unbroken metres which Watts had to discipline. Wesley found that work done for him. The wonder is not that Watts is, when compared with Wesley, rough and grotesque, but that he has achieved even his moderate success in harnessing his verse to his theology. Here is an example at random from Psalm xx: 'Some trust in chariots and some in horses: but we will remember the name of the Lord our God'. The Scottish version is:

> In chariots some put confidence,
>   Some horses trust upon;
> But we remember will the name
>   Of our Lord God alone.

Watts writes:

> Some trust in horses train'd for war,
> And some of chariots make their boasts;
> Our surest expectations are
> From Thee, the Lord of heav'nly hosts.

I have not chosen a grotesque, but an average, passage. But you can see Watts smoothing the verses down. In the eighteenth century they will be smoothed quite flat.

From the seventeenth century Watts derived another quality which makes him very unlike Wesley. This quality reminds us of Milton, even though the difference between Milton and Watts is very great. Let me put it this way. Charles Wesley in his hymns concerns himself mainly (I had almost written exclusively) with God and the soul of man: their manifold relations, their estrangement, their reconciliation, their union. Watts, too, concerns himself with this drama; but he gives it a cosmic background. Not less than Wesley, he finds the Cross the centre of his thought: all things look forward or backward to the Incarnation and the Passion. But Watts sees the Cross, as Milton had seen it, planted on a globe hung in space; surrounded by the vast distances of the universe. He sees the drama in Palestine prepared before the beginning of time and still decisive when time has ceased to be. There is a sense of the spaciousness of nature, of the vastness of time, of the dreadfulness of eternity, in Watts which is missing or less felt in Wesley. You have a touch of it in the last verse of Watts's greatest and best-known hymn, 'When I survey'. 'Were *the whole realm of nature* mine': the whole realm of Nature—no thought, no expression is more characteristic of Watts than that. It is an echo of his encyclopaedic philosophic thought. You constantly find Watts 'surveying' the whole realm of Nature and finding at the centre of it its crucified and dying Creator.

In the most hideous period of the last war, in a rather dingy, dreary chapel in the Potteries, I heard Dr. F. B. Meyer preach (as only he could) on the Passion. He took for his text Watts's hymn 'When I survey'; and to this day I can give you the headings and gist of that moving sermon. I recall what Dr. Meyer said about the word 'survey': a cold, rather formal word for the sinner's looking at the Saviour, he thought it, but it was (he admitted) very characteristic of Watts. It is the word of a man who, in seventeenth-century fashion, sees the world in a grain of sand and eternity in an hour. John Bailey says that in no poet are we so frequently made aware of the sky as in Milton. In this Watts is Milton's disciple. The spaciousness of the firmament is always appearing in his hymns, and he cannot glance or look at so vast an expanse of time and space as the scene of our redemption unfolds: he must *survey* it.

> Ere the blue heavens were stretched abroad
> From everlasting was the Word.

There is a magical quality in that verse. Watts knows that the 'blue heavens' alone provide an adequate background for any thought of the Word. It is like Milton. It is like Dante. It has sublimity. That sublimity was partly lost in the intense examination of the human soul which marked the evangelical and pietist movements, but in Watts it leads straight to the Calvinist's awareness of the sovereignty of God.

> God is a name my soul adores
>   The almighty Three, the eternal One;
> Nature and grace, with all their powers,
>   Confess the Infinite unknown.
>
> Thy voice produced the sea and spheres,
>   Bade the waves roar, the planets shine;
> But nothing like Thyself appears
>   Through all these spacious works of Thine.
>
> Still restless nature dies and grows,
>   From change to change the creatures run;
> Thy being no succession knows,
>   And all Thy vast designs are one.
>
> A glance of Thine runs through the globe,
>   Rules the bright worlds, and moves their frame;
> Of light Thou form'st Thy dazzling robe,
>   Thy ministers are living flame.
>
> How shall polluted mortals dare
>   To sing Thy glory or Thy grace?
> Beneath Thy feet we lie afar,
>   And see but shadows of Thy face.

> Who can behold the blazing light?
>   Who can approach consuming flame?
> None but Thy wisdom knows Thy might,
>   None but Thy word can speak Thy name.

These verses, though less august, show the same perception of the great realm of Nature:

> Firm are the words His prophets give,
> Sweet words, on which his children live;
> Each of them is the voice of God
> Who spoke and spread the skies abroad.
>
> Each of them powerful as the sound
> That bid the new-made world go round;
> And stronger than the solid poles
> On which the wheel of nature rolls.
>
> O for a strong, a lasting faith
> To credit what my Maker saith,
> T' embrace the message of His Son
> And call the joys of heaven our own!
>
> *Then*, should the earth's old pillars shake
> And all the wheels of nature break,
> Our steady souls should fear no more
> Than solid rocks when billows roar.
>
> Our everlasting hopes arise
> Above the ruinable skies,
> Where the eternal Builder reigns,
> And His own courts His power sustains.

It is not, I think, an accident that the Methodists have drawn so freely on this type of hymn by Watts. Charles Wesley himself provided them with ample riches in the expression of evangelical faith; but the genius which presided over the evolution of the Methodist hymn-book consciously or unconsciously understood that Watts could supplement Wesley on this other side. In this way it has come about that the Methodists have a splendid store of Watts's hymns on what we may pretentiously call the cosmic setting of the Faith. They have valued Watts in some ways more than we.

The verses that I last quoted contain two interesting words from which we may now jump to consider Watts's diction. Did you note the fine phrase 'above the ruinable skies'? Watts has a flair for the use of the memorable word. We shall find that as we proceed. The other word is 'old': 'should the earth's old pillars shake'. Unless you are very careful, that sounds ludicrous. We want Watts to say 'ancient' or to use a more dignified word. 'Old' is a word that has lost caste since 1709. Compare

> The sons of good old Jacob seem'd
> Abandon'd to their foes.

Unhappily for Watts, many of his words have lost caste; and verse after verse of his psalms and hymns we find ruined by a turn of phrase that, once venerable, is become comic. The great divide, I surmise, is somewhere near Addison. Words have changed less since then. That is why Wesley seems less archaic or 'dated' than Watts, though, of course, there are a few expressions in Wesley that strike us as odd. But there are many in Watts. Very much too often we descend from the sublime to the ridiculous with a shattering bump, or, when he wishes to move us he makes us squirm.

> Here every bowel of our God
> With soft compassion rolls.

Not merely by his fondness for 'bowels' and 'worms' does Watts disturb us, but by scores and scores of expressions that died in the polite reformation of Augustan English.

So much then we must expect for the simple but adequate reason that Watts's taste was formed in the seventeenth and not in the eighteenth century. As an example, let me quote Watts's use of the exclamation 'Well'. He is very fond of this, but it gives a grotesquely colloquial touch to some of his solemn passages. He is contrasting the eternal life of God with the transitoriness of His creatures.

> The sea and sky must perish too,
>   And vast destruction come;
> The creatures—look, how old they grow
>   And wait their fiery doom.

> Well, let the sea shrink all away
>   And flame melt down the skies;
> My God shall live an endless day
>   When th' old creation dies.

Or, in another sense, he opens a hymn:

> Well, the Redeemer's gone
>   T' appear before our God,
> To sprinkle o'er the flaming throne
>   With his atoning blood.

Or:

> Well, if our days must fly,
>   We'll keep their end in sight.

Bible readers will remember that the translators of the Authorized Version in their address to the Reader use 'Well' in a similar solemn manner. It is part of Watts's seventeenth-century inheritance.

I could fill pages with examples of this unhappy change in the meaning of Watts's words.

> Thou has redeem'd our souls from hell
>   With Thine *invaluable* blood.

> Yet with my God I leave my cause,
>   And trust His promised grace;
> He rules me by His *well-known* laws
>   Of love and righteousness.

> [God] rides upon the stormy sky
>   And *manages* the seas.

> Thee, mighty God, our souls *admire*.

> Must heaven's eternal *darling* die
> To save a trait'rous race?

> And Heaven without Thy presence there
> Would be a dark and *tiresome* place.

and, perhaps oddest of all,

> Through all His [God's] ancient works
> *Surprising* wisdom shines.

Examples leap from every page. These will suffice to explain why so many of Watts's hymns cannot be sung to-day.

At times it is not the odd word, but the quaint or crude thought which puts the psalm or hymn out of court. Watts out-Wordsworths Wordsworth in his love of simple, everyday language; and as Wordsworth at times made the sublime ridiculous by his kindergarten expressions so also did Watts. At its best Watts's language is pure and transparent. It is as pure Anglo-Saxon as Bunyan's own:

> Sweet fields beyond the swelling flood
> Stand dressed in living green.

But at its worst it is banal beyond belief. What modern versions of St. Paul's epistles have done for Romans and Ephesians Watts has done for the Psalms. The obscurity has gone: granted; but

so has the awe, the majesty, the numinous, the divine. Here is
a neutral example about manna:

> But they in murmuring language said,
>   'Manna is all our feast.
> We loathe this light, this airy bread,
>   We must have flesh to taste'.

> 'Ye shall have flesh to please your lust'
>   (The Lord in wrath replied)
> And sent them quails like sand or dust,
>   Heap'd up from side to side.

> He gave them all their own desire;
>   And greedy as they fed,
> His vengeance burnt with secret fire,
>   And smote the rebels dead.

And meritorious as Watts's use of Anglo-Saxon words is, free as
he is of pompous rubbish, his exclusion of Latin words deprives
him of those magical changes that Wesley knows so well how
to use. By the introduction of a word like 'essential' or 'transient' among Anglo-Saxon words Wesley will strike a deep note
in a way that holds you spell-bound. When he would be strong,
Watts is often merely violent.

At times, however, his violence becomes grand:

> They love the road that leads to hell;
>   Then let the rebels die
> Whose malice is implacable
>   Against the Lord on high.

> But if thou hast a chosen few
>   Amongst that impious race,
> Divide them from the bloody crew
>   By Thy surprising grace.

On Judgment Day:

> The angry nations fret and roar
> That they can slay the saints no more;
> On wings of vengeance flies our God
> To pay the long arrears of blood.

On Satan:

> Now Satan comes with dreadful roar,
>   And threatens to destroy;
> He worries whom he can't devour
>   With a malicious joy.

On the other hand, we have this pleasing picture of supernatural natural history:

> A thousand savage beasts of prey
>   Around the forest roam,
> But Judah's Lion guards the way
>   And guides the strangers home.

Here is the 'Warning to Magistrates,' to the Tory invaders of the rights of conscience who attempted to undermine the Toleration Act. It is worth the attention of Hitler:

> Yet you invade the rights of God,
> And send your bold decrees abroad
>   To bind the conscience in your chains.
>
> Break out their teeth, eternal God,
> Those teeth of lions dyed in blood,
>   And crush the serpents in the dust.
> As empty chaff, when whirlwinds rise,
> Before the sweeping tempest flies,
>   So let their hopes and names be lost.

But Watts was sometimes a master of understatement, as well as sometimes a slave of exaggeration. There is a neatness about this next verse which makes even *Esquire* seem cumbrous. Watts is writing on the excellency of the Christian religion:

> Not the feign'd fields of heathenish bliss
> Could raise such pleasures to the mind,
> Nor does the Turkish Paradise
> Pretend to joys so well-refined.

You notice that, even when he is most grotesque, he lets slip the great phrase. 'The feign'd fields of heathenish bliss' might be Milton. 'To pay the long arrears of blood' might be Shakespeare. Might it not be Aeschylus?

One other quality that has not helped the hymns demands a word. Watts, it must be confessed, is not always very clever at rhymes. Something must be allowed for changes in pronunciation of vowels and diphthongs. Something may be due to a faulty ear. But much, I am persuaded, is due to haste and carelessness. Have you noticed how many poor rhymes, false rhymes, and mere assonances occur even in his great hymns? Watts rarely tries to rhyme more than the second and fourth lines. That, to begin with, is letting himself off easily. Contrast Wesley, who usually rhymes first and third as well as second and fourth, and so gets a more compact verse. Take as an example 'Jesus shall reign'. In six verses, with twelve alleged rhymes, we find no fewer than five of the twelve imperfect. Watts is in this matter distinctly inferior to Wesley, who had, of course, a gifted musical ear and a rare facility in Latin verse to help him. Wesley's book, as well as Watts's, contains, of course, a good many false rhymes and mere assonances, but Wesley's do not weaken his verse as much as one would at first expect. This is because, unlike Watts, Wesley leaves very few lines without some attempt at rhyming. If lines 2 and 4 rhyme badly, lines 1 and 3 partly save the situation for Wesley. Watts has too often neglected to provide himself with this safety valve, and one bad rhyme, being the only rhyme, puts the verse out of action. So marked is the difference that if you read a hundred pages of Watts at a sitting, and come

(as you will come) on the hymn perfectly smoothed and perfectly rhymed, your inclination is to say, 'Why, Wesley might
have written that!' for at his best Watts is as accomplished as
Wesley.

I take two of Watts's smoothest examples. You will note how
much they gain because here, like Wesley, he sets out to rhyme
lines 1 and 3 as well as 2 and 4. Even here, however, Watts
does not give us perfect rhymes:

> Not all the outward forms on earth,
>   Nor rites that God has given,
> Nor will of man, nor blood, nor birth,
>   Can raise a soul to Heaven.
>
> The sovereign will of God alone
>   Creates us heirs of grace,
> Born in the image of His Son,
>   A new, peculiar race.

Or this:

> Nor eye has seen, nor ear has heard,
>   Nor sense, nor reason known,
> What joys the Father has prepared
>   For those that love the Son.

Each verse has one false and one true rhyme. Spread this defective rhyming equally all over the psalms and hymns and you see
the result is considerable and depressing.

You will perhaps assume from what I have said that the
common opinion is true, that our hymn-books have selected the
best of Watts, and that we are not missing much in missing all
but the twenty-five hymns or so with which we are familiar.
Let no word of mine lead you into that error. When every
deduction for every reason has been made, Watts's psalms and
hymns contain many, many pieces which would enrich our
worship. Not a few, it is true, contain a phrase or word that is
now comic or grotesque; but by no means all. And even those

hymns which, for such reasons, we cannot sing in public, we neglect at our peril in private. I at least know of no devotional book richer than Watts's hymns and psalms. The whole piece may be unfit for use, but the great phrase, the great thought, the penetrating analysis, the blinding flash of genius lighting up Calvary afresh for us—these things would purge and wring and subdue and elevate and all but save our souls, did we give them the chance. Watts's was a great mind, a great soul, a great experience. Much that he writes is too intimate except for the holy of holies. But we ought to use it there.

Every one will make his own selection. I should have been sorry to miss this meditation:

> Here at Thy cross, my dying God,
>   I lay my soul beneath Thy love.
>
> Not all that tyrants think, or say,
>   With rage and lightning in their eyes,
> Nor hell shall fright my heart away,
>   Should hell with all its legions rise,
>
> Should worlds conspire to drive me thence,
>   Moveless and firm this heart should lie,
> Resolv'd (for that's my last defence)
>   If I must perish, there to die.
>
> .   .   .   .   .
>
> There I behold, with sweet delight,
>   The blessed Three in One;
> And strong affections fix my sight
>   On God's incarnate Son.
>
> .   .   .   .   .
>
> And if no evening visit's paid
>   Between my Saviour and my soul,
> How dull the night, how sad the shade,
>   How mournfully the minutes roll.
>
> .   .   .   .   .

Deep in our hearts let us record
The deeper sorrows of our Lord.

. . . . .

The mount of danger is the place
Where we shall see·surprising grace.

. . . . .

Turn, turn us, mighty God,
    And mould our souls afresh;
Break, sovereign grace, these hearts of stone,
    And give us hearts of flesh.

It is time, after examining the limitations, to observe the
strong features of Watts's verse. We have glanced at the simple
Anglo-Saxon words which compose it. Page after page shows
no Latin word. Whole verses are in monosyllables. The
experiment is too difficult to succeed always, but if it comes off
it is heavenly in its clarity and light. You can notice this in
everything that I quote from Watts.

There are few tricks in Watts's verse, but he is fond of some
simple devices. These interest us because first we can watch him
practising them in scores of feeble or moderate verses, and then
using them to bring off some distinguished performance in a
classic hymn.

He is very fond, for instance, of a sort of repetition or parallelism. This descends perhaps from his putting into verse so
many of the parallel sentences of Hebrew poetry. At times he
repeats an idea, at times a phrase, at times only a word.

Down to the earth was Satan thrown,
Down to the earth his legions fell,
High on the cross the Saviour hung,
High in the heavens He reigns.

To Jesus our atoning Priest,
To Jesus our superior King.

I'll make your great commission known,
    And ye shall prove my gospel true
By all the works that I have done,
    By all the wonders ye shall do.

A more interesting type is here:

> He bids the sun forbear to rise,
> Th' obedient sun forbears.

In the creation:

> 'Let blood,' He said, 'flow round the veins,'
> And round the veins it flows.

Note the chiasmus there too.

> Our days alas! our mortal days
> Are short and wretched too;
> 'Evil and few,' the patriarch says,
> And well the patriarch knew.

Watts is particularly fond of pairing his lines in a way of his own. Most writers pair lines 1 and 2 or 3 and 4, and Watts often does that too. But he very often secures an interesting effect by pairing lines 2 and 3:

> Nor shall Thy spreading Gospel rest
> Till through the world Thy truth has run,
> Till Christ has all the nations bless'd
> That see the light or feel the sun.

> Down to this base, this sinful earth,
> He came to raise our nature high;
> He came t' atone almighty wrath;
> Jesus, the God, was born to die.

Not very remarkable, you may say. Wait a moment. Turn now to the greatest of Watts's hymns, and see this particular form of parallelism, combined with a chiasmus, in the second and third lines of the verse. See Watts bring off with apparently artless art the performance for which he has practised scores and scores of times:

> See from His head, His hands, His feet,
>   Sorrow and love flow mingled down.
> Did e'er such love and sorrow meet,
>   Or thorns compose so rich a crown?

Another device of which Watts is very fond is accumulation. He piles up words and ideas of the same order, and produces the effect memorably described in Burke's treatise, *On the Sublime and Beautiful*:

> His worship and his fear shall last
> Till hours and years and time be past.

> . . . . .

> (There Persia, glorious to behold,
> There India shines in eastern gold)
> And barb'rous nations at His word
> Submit and bow and own their Lord.

> . . . . .

> No bleeding bird, nor bleeding beast,
> Nor hyssop branch, nor sprinkling priest,
> Nor running brook, nor flood, nor sea,
> Can wash the dismal stain away.

Sometimes Watts accumulates phrases, as when Wisdom speaks:

> Before the flying clouds,
>   Before the solid land,
> Before the fields, before the floods,
>   I dwelt at His right hand.

Not much in it? Perhaps not; but, for all that, you will find it a feature of the greatest of his hymns:

> See from His head, His hands, His feet.

> . . . . .

> While life and thought and being last,
>   Or immortality endures.

> . . . . .

> While such as trust their native strength
> Shall melt away and droop and die.

From Milton, I suspect, Watts learnt his mastery of proper names. They adorn his verse frequently and happily. Sometimes they strike us as odd.

> He takes my soul ere I'm aware,
> And shows me where His glories are;
> No chariot of Amminadib
> The heavenly rapture can describe.

Or:

> So Samson, when his hair was lost,
> Met the Philistines to his cost,
> Shook his vain limbs with sad surprise,
> Made feeble fight, and lost his eyes.

But this is impressive:

> What mighty man, or mighty God,
>   Comes travelling in State
> Along the Idumæan road
>   Away from Bozrah's gate?

And have you noticed the triumph of long practice with proper names in 'There is a land of pure delight'? In one couplet Watts works off three of them. We do not notice them as heavy or precious; and yet they awaken that historic memory which only proper names can command:

> So to the Jews old Canaan stood,
>   While Jordan roll'd between.

Watts has achieved perfect mastery when he can use proper names to bewitch us without our noticing it.

You remember that other quality which we observed earlier: Watts's awareness of the whole universe as the setting for human life and for the drama of salvation. That quality gives deep tones to his greatest hymns. That, too, he controls after much experiment. I need only remind you of

Time, like an ever-rolling stream.

.   .   .   .   .

The busy tribes of flesh and blood,
  With all their lives and cares,
Are carried downwards by the flood
  And lost in following years.

.   .   .   .   .

The Mighty God, whose matchless power
  Is ever new and ever young,
And firm endures while endless years
  Their everlasting circles run.

And of course supremely:

Were the whole realm of nature mine.

Watts, then, achieves his supreme triumphs not by accident.
They are compounded of many ingredients already well known
to him, experimented with happily and unhappily, carelessly as
well as carefully, but finally subdued by his art in a classic hymn.
For some of the hymns as whole pieces, notably for 'When I
survey' and for 'There is a land', we can find rough drafts in
his book.

We have lingered perhaps too long on the lesser things. Let
me ask a final question touching greater matters than diction
and versification. What of Watts's choice of subjects? What
are the psalms and hymns about?

They concern, as is natural, some things of passing or historic
interest. In making David speak like a Christian, Watts most
properly made him speak also like an Englishman, not to say like
an eighteenth-century Whig. Watts equates, that is to say,
Palestine, Israel, Judea, Jerusalem with Great Britain. The
exquisitely sensitive commentators call this vulgar. Vulgar or
not, Watts does it. The result is that he gives us some fascina-
ting reflexions on English history. The deliverances of the
chosen people had their parallels in Gunpowder Plot, the land-
ing of William of Orange, the accession of George I, and

generally in the defeat of the French, the discomfiture of the
Tories, and the confusion of the Papists. 'Popish idolatry
reproved: a psalm for the 5th of November'; 'The church saved
and her enemies disappointed: composed for the 5th of November, 1694'; 'Power and government from God alone: applied to
the Glorious Revolution by King William or the happy accession of King George to the throne'. The hymns are full of
sound political doctrine as well as thanksgiving.

> Britain was doomed to be a slave,
>   Her frame dissolved, her fears were great.
> When God a new supporter gave
>   To bear the pillars of the State.
>
>   .   .   .   .   .
>
> No vain pretence to royal birth
>   Shall fix a tyrant on the throne.

The lesson is clear:

> Oft has the Lord whole nations bless'd
>   For His own church's sake;
> The pow'rs that give His people rest
>   Shall of His care partake.
>
>   .   .   .   .   .
>
> Let Cæsar's due be ever paid
>   To Cæsar and his throne,
> But consciences and souls were made
>   To be the Lord's alone.

Here is Guy Fawkes:

> Their secret fires in caverns lay,
>   And we the sacrifice;
> But gloomy caverns strove in vain
>   To 'scape all searching eyes.
>
> Their dark designs were all revealed,
>   Their treason all betray'd.

But nevertheless:

> In vain the busy sons of hell
> Still new rebellions try.

The grandson of Blake's lieutenant rejoices in the success of our arms, in the cause of liberty and Protestantism:

> How have we chas'd them through the field,
> And trod them to the ground,
> While Thy salvation was our shield,
> But they no shelter found.
>
> .   .   .   .   .
>
> In vain to idol saints they cry,
> And perish in their blood.

The decline of the Dissenting interest in the early eighteenth century has left a pathetic reflexion in Watts. Empty churches are not new phenomena.

> 'Tis with a mournful pleasure now
> I think on ancient days;
> Then to Thy house did numbers go,
> And all our work was praise.
> In God they boasted all the day,
> And in a cheerful throng
> Did thousands meet to praise and pray,
> And grace was all their song.
>
> But now our souls are seiz'd with shame,
> Confusion fills our face.
>
> .   .   .   .   .
>
> Yet have we not forgot our God,
> Nor falsely dealt with heav'n.

Most of the psalms and hymns contain no local or passing reference. They deal—ninety-nine out of a hundred of them— with the great elemental facts that always dominate the Christian's mind. There is indeed a certain sameness about Watts's

book because he deals so constantly with the same three or four
topics. There is nothing denominational about him. We find
rather less reflexion of the intense fellowship of classic Congregationalism than we should have expected. Watts deals with
the great common themes of catholic Christianity.

There is, to begin with, the most frank and most moving
recital of the weakness, the unsatisfactoriness, the transience of
human life. The hopes and fears of men Watts portrays with a
tender but unflinching hand. No man has analysed more faithfully the doubts and hopes and fears that we all have.

> The passions of my hope and fear
> Maintain'd a doubtful strife,
> While sorrow, pain, and sin conspir'd
> To take away my life.

And all is set over against the vast universe:

> Like flowery fields the nations stand,
> Pleas'd with the morning light;
> The flow'rs beneath the mower's hand
> Lie with'ring ere 'tis night.

Watts is almost Virgilian in this. Not less than Virgil, he
deserves Tennyson's great word:

> Thou majestic in thy sadness
> At the doubtful doom of human kind.

There is no easy sentimentality in Watts. He has one foot firmly
on earth. His quite ghastly poems about death and the grave,
about Hell and Satan, provide valuable evidence that he at
least had allowed for the emergence of Mussolini and Hitler.
Watts is a sound Calvinist. He knows that mankind has fallen.
He takes full note of evil, and allows handsomely for it.

But if one of Watts's feet is firmly planted on earth, the other is no less firmly planted on catholic, evangelical, apostolic theology. A line which, for another purpose, I have already quoted gives us in strong epigrammatic form the other thing which Watts sees over against the tragedy of human life:

> Jesus, the God, was born to die.

In its blazing antitheses: the Galilean carpenter who is God: the God who is born: the God who dies; it carries us back to the most ancient hymns of the Greek and the Latin Church.

> Our souls adore th' Eternal God,
> Who condescended to be born.

The Incarnation, the Passion, the Resurrection—these things are for Watts no less certain than the frustration of human hopes. That is why (in his own word) he is, on the balance, 'cheerful'.

> Till God in human form I see
>   My thoughts no comfort find.
>
> .   .   .   .   .
>
> But if Immanuel's face I see
>   My hope, my joy begins.
>
> I love th' incarnate mystery
>   And there I place my trust.

Here is the final vision of a Love of God older than the universe and filling it:

> So strange, so boundless was the love
>   That pitied dying men,
> The Father sent His equal Son
>   To give them life again.
>
> 'Christ be my first elect,' He said,
> Then chose our souls in Christ our head,
> Before He gave the mountains birth
> Or laid foundations for the earth.

Thus did eternal love begin
To raise us up from death and sin;
Our characters were then decreed
'Blameless in love, a holy seed.'

So let our lips and lives express
That holy gospel we profess.

Now by the bowels of my God,
    His sharp distress, His sore complaints,
By His last groans, His dying blood,
    I charge my soul to love the saints.

Tender and kind be all our thoughts,
    Through all our lives let mercy run;
So God forgives our numerous faults
    For the dear sake of Christ His Son.

These are the august notes of true Catholic theology and true
Christian living. I know of no better introduction to classical
theology than Watts. Let me give you two examples. Recently
I read through the Gloss Ordinary and the other main com-
mentaries used by medieval theologians on the first few chapters
of the Song of Solomon. I found it again almost word for word
in Watts's paraphrases of that book. And in Watts's 'Jesus
shall reign' you have the great verse (omitted, of course, nowadays from our books because it is so great):

In Him [Christ] the sons of Adam boast
More blessings than their father lost.

What is that but the glorious passage from the ancient Office
for Easter Eve? 'O certainly necessary sin of Adam . . . O
happy fault which deserved to have such and so great a Re-
deemer.'

Watts's book moves to a splendid end in his sacramental
hymns. The Lord's Supper has an essential place in Watts's
religion.

> I love the Lord, who stoops so low
>   To give His word a seal.
> And thus our sense assists our faith[1]
>   And shows us what His gospel means.

He sets out the high sacramental doctrine of the Savoy Confession. The Lord's Supper is more than a memorial.

> This holy bread and wine
>   Maintains our fainting breath
> By union with our living Lord
>   And interest in His death.

> Here have we seen Thy face, O Lord,
>   And view'd salvation with our eyes;
> Tasted and felt the Living Word,
>   The bread descending from the skies.

He remembers with infinite tenderness those who once partook with us of the Supper here on earth.

> While once upon this lower ground,
>   Weary and faint ye stood,
> What dear refreshments here ye found
>   From this immortal food.

> Here God's whole name appears complete,
>   Nor wit can guess, nor reason prove,
> Which of the letters best is writ,
>   The power, the wisdom, or the love.

If I were asked to compare Watts with Wesley in a word, I should say, I think, though with great diffidence, that Watts seems to me to have the greater mind, the wider outlook, the

---

[1] St. Thomas Aquinas has the complementary thought in his great eucharistic hymn, *Pange, lingua:*

> Praestet fides supplementum
> Sensuum defectui.

more philosophic approach to human life and to the Christian revelation. He has also, I think, more original poetry in him. Now and then he hits out a greater and more elemental phrase than any that I remember in Wesley. But Wesley is the greater artist. He flies more surely. He crashes far less often. He reaches the heights far more often, though perhaps he does not go quite as high. His book, as a whole, far surpasses Watts. Watts, because he is dominated by the notion of paraphrasing, puts Scripture very often into his own words; it is not always to the advantage of Scripture. Wesley does little paraphrasing. He puts his own notions into Scripture language, and it is always to their advantage. Each is scriptural; they are equally scriptural, but in different ways, and the literary luck is with Wesley. Watts had it in him to do better than Wesley ever did, better than he himself ever did.

But in essentials they are one; and they provide us with one quite conclusive reason for being Christians as far as we can be. They form a heritage that only a madman will let slip. Let Watts have the last word in the last lines of his superb doxology to the Holy Trinity:

> Where reason fails,
>   With all her powers,
> There faith prevails
>   And love adores.

Mɪss Rose Macaulay has now attained that age, or that circulation, at which popular novelists become omniscient; and like others of her class in that condition she has tried her prentice hand on religion. Works on *The Outline of History* and *How to Reconstruct Europe* will follow, no doubt: but the attraction of a religious subject is such that only the very shrewd can resist attacking it first. In an article on 'How to Choose a Religion', as I expect you know, Miss Macaulay lately displayed all that ignorance of essential detail which Mr. Wells has taught us to associate with omniscience. In the course of some not unpleasing observations on the several sects of Christendom, Miss Macaulay speaks of the Greek Church as if it had not revised its calendar; she flounders in a vain effort to distinguish Presbyterianism and Calvinism; she says that the ugliest building in a village is sure to be the chapel, obviously forgetting that, true as this may have been in her youth, village halls have been built since; she adds that Unitarianism is a suitable religion for people who cannot believe much; when, as everyone knows, the precise opposite is true: Unitarianism asking people to believe all the most improbable part of Christian doctrine after removing all the reasons that begin to make it credible.

But if you shy long enough, you are sure to hit something sooner or later, and Miss Macaulay has observed accurately one thing; she says that if ever you pass a Wesleyan or Baptist or Congregational chapel you will hear hymn-singing proceeding inside. She argues therefore that among us orthodox Dissenters, as distinct from the more fancy varieties, hymns take a great part in divine service. And here at least she is right; and that is why it is seemly that you should hear a paper on hymns, even if it be less certain that I can appropriately read it.

[1] A paper read before the Cambridge University Congregational Society in the Easter term, 1924.

For let me confess at the beginning that I have no special qualification and several special disqualifications for speaking about hymns. I lay claim at once to every kind of musical ignorance, doubting sometimes if I can go even as far as Dr. Johnson in calling music the least unpleasant of noises. I do not study, nor even possess, that book without which no student of hymns can allow himself to be, Julian's *Dictionary of Hymnology*. I have drawn up no statistical tables of authors, centuries, denominations, and subjects. I know about hymns only what any one must know who for a quarter of a century has been so addicted to chapel-going as to attend service twice every Sunday. I think I never sing a hymn without discovering who wrote it, and after doing this some scores of times I usually end by remembering. No particular credit is due to any of us who does this, for most hymn-books now have a list of authors and their dates somewhere. These details may have been supposed to interfere with the devotion of singers in times when denominational feeling ran high. They were suppressed, therefore, or relegated to decent obscurity in out-of-the-way indexes. It was doubtless by the use of this holy cunning that Methodists were induced to sing 'Rock of Ages' with a clear and happy conscience though its author, Toplady, had called John Wesley 'a low and puny tadpole in divinity', 'actuated by Satanic shamelessness and Satanic guilt'.

To-day, when the orthodox will sing hymns by Unitarians and Theosophists without turning a hair, these precautions are, it may be supposed, unnecessary. The *Methodist Hymn-book* issued in 1904 goes farther than names and dates. It adds biographical notes, often useful, often irrelevant, always interesting, and sometimes wrong. On what principle the Wesleyan Conference selected its information I defy any one to pronounce. When all else fails, the birthplace appears—quite often alone: *born at Brighton; born in London; born at Bath*. Of Philip Bliss we learn only that he was an American killed on a railway; of Monsell that he was killed during the rebuilding of his church at Guildford; of Sears, the author of 'It came upon the midnight clear', it is a relief to learn that, though a Unitarian minister, he 'held always to the absolute divinity of Christ'; but when I am told of W. C. Dix, who wrote 'As with gladness men of old', that 'from thirty to forty of his hymns are in common use', I can only decline to believe it; for I never knew any one who has even heard of half a dozen.

I am, nevertheless, very grateful for that Methodist Biographical Index. I have spent many happy hours in research into it; and sometimes the researcher comes on a treasure. I always loved James Montgomery; but I felt as if I knew him when I read that he was the son of a Moravian minister, lived in Sheffield for sixty-two years, edited the *Sheffield Iris*, and recited 'Hail to the Lord's Anointed, Great David's greater Son', at a Wesleyan Missionary Meeting in Liverpool in 1822. I can only be sorry for the people who do not know that; I can only be angry with the people who are not moved by the picture of the Editor of the *Sheffield Iris* reciting that splendid hymn. And yet, despite the riches of this sort that it brings us, we remember with a pang that this same Biographical Index in the new *Methodist Hymn-book* replaces that splendid single telling sentence in the old one: 'Where no name is given it may be assumed that the hymn is the work of Mr. Charles Wesley.'

You will gather that the *Methodist Hymn-book* of 1904 is one of the hymn books I claim to know tolerably. The other is Dr. Barrett's *Hymnal*. These I know from constant use; others from casual use. Adventures at holiday times have made me almost too familiar with *Worship Song*; and a kinder fate, in remote Lincolnshire, often showed me the old *Congregational Hymn-book*. With Presbyterian and Baptist books I have but a conventional acquaintance; with *Ancient and Modern* and the *English Hymnal* a better but not exhaustive one.

That, then, is my stock in trade. My method is this: to avoid wandering aimlessly in generalizations, I shall take the book that I know best—Dr. Barrett's—and examine it in some detail. I shall notice the several elements of which it is composed. I shall notice how far Dr. Barrett modified these. I shall notice what changes have come over popular feeling for hymns since Dr. Barrett made his selection. By taking a firm stand on Dr. Barrett's book, we shall secure, at least, a point of vantage from which we can survey the wild scene that the title of my paper conjures up.

But before I speak of Dr. Barrett's book, I propose to lay down two canons which govern all my thought and treatment of the subject.

First, I think it improper to criticize hymns as if they were ordinary verses: to say of any hymn it is 'not poetry' or it is 'poor poetry' is to say nothing. A hymn—a good hymn—is not necessarily poetry of any sort, good or bad: just as poetry, good or bad, is not necessarily a hymn. A hymn like 'Jesu, Lover of my soul', may be poor religious poetry: but, in face of its place in English religion, only imbecility will declare it a poor hymn. George Herbert wrote much excellent religious poetry, but it may be doubted if he wrote one tolerable hymn. Hymns do not form a subdivision of poetry. They are a distinct kind of composition, neither prose nor poetry: they are, in a word, hymns; and I refuse to be drawn any nearer than that to a definition. A hymn may be poetry as it may be theology. It is not, of necessity, either.

Second, reverence is due to hymns as to any sacred object. The hymn that revolts me, if it has been a means of grace to Christian men, I must respect as I should respect a communion cup, however scratched its surface, however vulgar its decoration. The bad jokes about hymns which newspapers publish in chatty columns by 'Uncle Remus' or 'Everyman in Town' are, apart from their intrinsic feebleness, an offence against my second canon.

Dr. Barrett's *Hymnal*, the Preface tells us, took its origin from a resolution of the Congregational Union, passed forty years ago. It was published in 1887. It held the field till 1916, when, as far as I can make out, the *Congregational Hymnary* appeared, though perhaps characteristically the Congregational

Union Committee neglected to date their work. The epitaph which the Committee wrote for Dr. Barrett's book, was: 'It is not possible to form any adequate estimate of the great influence of this book.' It is rash to go farther than a Committee, but I will suggest that Dr. Barrett's book is eminent as an exposition of what is best in Congregationalism. It reflects purely and clearly that mind which we should like to think is the Congregational mind: in taste, catholic; in feeling, evangelical; in expression, scholarly; in doctrine, orthodox. It is a book free from fads, fancies, prejudices, party slogans; taking the best from whatever source; most Congregational in lacking the denominationally Congregational note; a simply Christian book. Sweet reasonableness, sweetness and light—these are its characteristics: and, if we must criticize, these are its weaknesses. You feel at times, when you are hypercritical (but only then), that it is too sweetly reasonable and that all the corners have been too carefully removed. The atmosphere is so undisturbed that you crave for almost any impurity, any smell of human kind, any passion, any flaring, roaring enthusiasm. The crooked has been made too straight, the rough places too plain. It is just a little too well-behaved, but the fault is hardly there; for, if you look again, you see that this same book, for all its good behaviour, contains the most passionate pleading of the evangelical revival, 'Stay, thou insulted Spirit, stay', and the agonized prayer of the Chartist, 'When wilt Thou save the people? O God of mercy, when?'

Dr. Barrett achieved this result because he allowed no variety of religious experience known in 1887 to escape his notice. He laid under contribution every age, every nation, every communion.

It is worth while to disentangle the threads which Dr. Barrett wove together; or, if we change the figure, to trace back to their sources separated in time and space the several streams that met in 1887. There were, to begin with, those two great movements of English religion, the Oxford and the Evangelical. Both Dr. Barrett boldly claimed for us; and he was so happily placed that he could draw from each its maximum contribution.

For consider first the Oxford Movement. In 1887 the Oxford Movement had made almost all the valuable, original contributions it was to make to English religion. It was still a virile and scholarly movement; it had not yet sunk to sentimentality and fanaticism. How much of the Oxford Movement there is in the *Hymnal*, I doubt if most of you have noticed. The influence is twofold. There are, first, the hymns of the Oxford Movement men themselves. Keble gave us some of our best: 'O timely happy, timely wise', 'Sun of my soul', 'When God of old came down from heaven' (of which more later) and 'There is a book who runs may read'. Newman gave us two: 'Lead, kindly Light, and 'Praise to the Holiest'. Faber has more room than either Keble or Newman, and, of course, has too much: he passed from the sublime to the ridiculous too easily. 'Sweet Saviour, bless us ere we go', and 'O come and mourn with me awhile', and 'Was there ever kindest Shepherd' show us Faber at his best. Even in these there is a strain of weakness that develops in other hymns until it can hardly be borne. The pruning knife could be used nowhere with better effect than among the Faber hymns. We may set beside these writers W. C. Dix, with his 'As with gladness men of old' for Epiphany, 'To Thee, O Lord, our hearts we raise' for Harvest, and 'Come unto Me, ye weary', for all times. 'As with gladness men of old' is a model of straight, clear, clean verse.

But beside these and other hymns written by the men of the Movement, we owe to it an even greater debt for its inspiration of translation. The translations in Barrett's book fall into two main classes: the pietist hymns of Germany and the Greek and Latin hymns recovered by the Oxford Movement. Greatest among translators is John Mason Neale, though his rugged verse gave much opportunity and some excuse for the art of the amender. The unimaginative editors of *Ancient and Modern* scattered his remains pitilessly over their pages. 'O come, O come, Emmanuel, 'All glory, laud, and honour', 'O happy band of pilgrims', 'Art thou weary', 'The day is past and over', 'The day of resurrection', and the magnificent poem of Bernard of Cluny on the heavenly Jerusalem which we know as 'Brief life is here our portion' and 'Jerusalem the golden'; these and many others Barrett used. Barrett gave us so many that we are left gasping at his omission of one of Neale's best, glorious with the fresh triumph of Easter morning, 'The foe behind, the deep before'. We should have been only more surprised if the new *Hymnary* had repaired Barrett's mistake. Caswall, though a smaller man than Neale, did first-rate translations which Barrett used. 'Jesus, the very thought of Thee', and that moving Christmas hymn, adorable in its austere and primitive piety, 'Hark, an awful voice is sounding'—these stand as types.

Much as English hymn-singers owe to the Oxford Movement, they owe more to the Evangelical Revival. The Evangelical Revival was a religious movement not less deep than the Oxford Movement, and almost the whole of its artistic expression is to be found in hymns. Hymns, on the other hand, were but one of the interests of the Oxford Movement, and not its greatest. Liturgy, church furniture, and architecture drew off a part of its artistic energy; but hymns had no competitors among the Evangelicals. To take out of Barrett's book the hymns of the five men, John and Charles Wesley, Newton, Cowper, and Montgomery—though it would not fully represent the contribution of the Evangelical Revival—would at least show how huge and how valuable the contribution was.

No selection of Wesley's hymns can satisfy (to say nothing of pleasing) any one who knows Wesley's own book, that 'little body of experimental and practical divinity', of which John Wesley might well inquire: 'In what other publication of the kind have you so distinct and full an account of scriptural Christianity? such a declaration of the heights and depths of religion, speculative and practical? so strong cautions against the most plausible errors, particularly those that are now most prevalent?' To find a parallel, we must go to the *Book of Common Prayer*. Wesley's book, like the Prayer Book, is a unity.

Though extracts may be useful and must be made, they are only fragments, and we want the whole. For a selection, Barrett's is good, and we leave it at that.

Of Cowper and Newton, I have been told, and am willing to believe, that Barrett chose all that was valuable and most that was tolerable. He did not overdo either, as he overdid Faber. But it is when we come to Montgomery that we see our debt most plainly. The more Montgomery is read the more his solid merit appears. It is a merit that is easily missed, for it has no showiness to recommend it. Barrett has nowhere shown his genius more; he made no mistakes in selecting from Montgomery, and any one who compares his selection with that made by the Methodists in 1904 will see at once Barrett's superiority. They score only in one place: they add, what Barrett omitted, the exquisite Communion hymn, 'Be known to us in breaking bread'.

The Evangelical Revival gave more than the hymns of the Wesleys, Cowper, Newton, and Montgomery, but we proceed to the third great stream that came out of the past. This is the school of the elder Dissent, drawing its origin from the metrical Psalms and versions of Scripture that arose in Reformation times. One of the best known is one of the earliest: 'All people that on earth do dwell' is the 100th Psalm in an Elizabethan version. In the times when every gentleman wrote verses, most divines wrote scriptural paraphrases and the energetic versified the whole Psalter. Here was the foundation of Doddridge's and Watts's hymns—a metrical Psalter with other paraphrases first, and then hymns for several occasions. The peculiar genius of Watts and Doddridge displayed itself in allegorizing the Psalms and the Old Testament generally in a Christian fashion. Doddridge, for example, turned Malachi's account of the profaning of the Lord's Table into a Communion hymn, 'My God, and is Thy table spread?' and Watts made David speak like a Christian. Barrett broke away from the old Dissenting tradition of prefacing hymns proper by a metrical Psalter, and in his reaction from the tradition he used perhaps less of the paraphrases than will satisfy posterity. It is easy to forget that the Scottish Metrical Version is only one among many. That version approved by the Church of Scotland had many parallels in English Dissent until the Evangelical Revival, by suddenly enriching and enlarging the small section of hymns, made hymns first overshadow and then eject the metrical Psalms.

Of the hymns written by Watts and Doddridge, Barrett preserved but a tiny number. But it is not possible to regret so acutely what is omitted from these two writers as we regret the Wesley omissions. Though Watts, at times, probably excels Charles Wesley's best, the general mass of verse falls well below Wesley's average; and Doddridge, in the mass, is rather worse than Watts. Doddridge and Watts present more flank for attack than Charles Wesley presents. They stick less closely to scriptural ideas and language, and more often deserve the censure of John Wesley's adjective, 'turgid'. But, when all is said, they are the crowning glory of Independent hymnology, and the suppression of the hymn, 'I'll praise my Maker while I've breath', by the *Congregational Hymnary* is not only a vice, but an unnatural vice. Congregationalists so disloyal to their spiritual progenitors deserve to be admitted at once to some reunion of Churches.

These, then, were the three main contributions which history made to Dr. Barrett's book—the Oxford Movement, the Evangelical Revival, and the elder Dissent. The fourth contribution came from the contemporary or almost contemporary mass of writers whose work was not specially or obviously stamped by any of these schools. By his contemporaries, Dr. Barrett, like the rest of us, was over-impressed. He took them too seriously and ranked them too highly, as we all do. And if the Congregational Union had to busy itself about hymns, the most useful revision of Barrett's book that it might have done was the elimination of the unfit of the nineteenth century, not the bowdlerization and decimation of the classics and the handing round of doles to doubtful contemporaries of our own.

But although there is decidedly too much of it, contemporary hymnology provided Dr. Barrett with some good things. First we notice the honourable place taken by three of our own communion—Josiah Conder, Thomas Hornblower Gill, and George Rawson. Conder was a true poet, himself an editor of hymn-books, who did in truth amend when he altered. One hymn of his, even if he had written nothing else, would place him in the first rank: I mean, of course, 'Bread of heaven, on Thee I feed'. Another Communion hymn, 'By Christ redeemed, in Christ restored', would do the same for Rawson. Gill wrote nothing quite so good; and both his fame and Rawson's would benefit by the suppression of not less than 50 per cent. of their *Hymnal* hymns.

Less good than these, as he is even more voluble, is Horatius Bonar, a useful, pedestrian sort of man who is never very good and not often very bad. He badly needs the pruning knife, but we may be grateful for 'I heard the voice of Jesus say' and 'O Love of God, how strong and true' and 'Fill Thou my life, O Lord my God'. Of Lynch and Lyte (except for 'Abide with me') not much good is to be said. Bickersteth, Monsell, Ellerton are a sort of Anglican Horatius Bonars. Heber provides better things; Grant and Thring worse. Mrs. Alexander is to be spoken of with affection as one of the simplest and purest of writers, but most of all because she wrote 'There is a green hill' and 'Once in royal David's city'. Much of Charlotte Elliott's verse has had its day, but some of us owe her eternal gratitude for 'Just as I am'. One great and typical Anglican hymn-writer in the last century was Bishop Walsham How. It might be respectably if not successfully maintained that he was, 'taking quantity and quality into consideration' (as the Methodist Index says of Charles Wesley), the greatest hymn-writer of the nineteenth century. Barrett used him much, but hardly too much. In Barrett's hands he is never bad, yet the Methodists contrived to find and print much rubbish by him. In 'O Word of God Incarnate', 'We give Thee but Thine own', 'O Jesus, Thou art standing', 'It is a thing most wonderful', he is almost great. That other voluminous episcopal composer, Bishop Wordsworth, Barrett sifted and winnowed many times, we may be sure, before he was able to present such good grain and so little chaff as his book contains.

Barrett, I said, had no fads. He did not, therefore, in the manner of modern compilers, scour the ends of the earth for heretical and pagan productions, but when a Quaker like Whittier, Unitarians like Oliver Wendell Holmes and Bowring, and heroes like Carlyle offered hymns, he took them.

Though I am sure it has been tedious, I am not sure that this part of my paper has been irrelevant, because it at least reminds you of the vastness and variety of the *corpus* of hymns with which modern Christendom has endowed itself; and it brings before us the material on which we may exercise our critical, appreciative, and discriminating faculties. Having made this outline survey of the result of Dr. Barrett's work, I want next to notice the principles on which the hymns were selected, rejected, and altered in 1887, and then to consider the change in principles which forty years have brought. Dr. Barrett gave out as some of his principles that his book 'should include some hymns which, though defective when tried by modern standards of taste and literary form, are yet closely connected with the history of the Evangelical faith in England, and with the spiritual experience of a large number of the members of Congregational churches; that it should give, wherever practicable, the original text of the hymns introduced. 'Some alterations have been admitted on the ground that they have been sanctioned by long and general use, and form part of the compositions in which they occur as generally known; and others (very few in number) in correction of minor irregularities of metre, offences against taste, or suggestions of questionable doctrine in the original text.'

As a general statement, that seems to me to contain correct doctrine. You must be preserved from the antiquarian peril. Hymns are for Christians, not for poets nor for antiquarians. One persistent trouble is that, having shut the door against

the poet, you find the antiquarian flying in at the window
—the antiquarian who demands the original text whatever
the cost in taste or style (which are small matters) or in
power to express real religious faith (which is a great
matter). A hymn's business is to strengthen the faith of
to-day, not to present an historical record of the faith of the
day before yesterday. That is not to say that hymns should
express only the sentiment and aspirations of the moment;
they should educate and purify faith, as well as record it; they
should be better than the singer. It is not, therefore, a sufficient
reason for scrapping a hymn that it is not written in the language
which the butcher, the baker, the candlestick-maker, or the
undergraduate would use to-day; its object is to make these
people speak and think differently. But to do this, though
removed from their vocabulary, it must be not too far removed.
It must not be out of reach, and mere antiquarianism must not
preserve what puts a hymn out of reach. Charles Wesley's
amazing verse may be criticized, for instance, as near the
boundary of pedantry and usefulness:

> Those amaranthine bowers
> (Unalienably ours)
> Bloom, our infinite reward,
>   Rise, our permanent abode;
> From the founded world prepared;
>   Purchased by the blood of God.

'The founded world' is indeed a pleasing Latinism, and congregations bred on such stuff should not suffer from flabbiness of
thought.

We now approach the problem of alterations. Let it be said
at once that Barrett was of all alterers the most honest: usually,
but not (I fear) always, he tells us the very line in which
an alteration occurs. His example did not suffice to maintain
this high standard in his successors. The editors of the *Hymnary*
say 'Altered' at the foot of the hymn, and try to hide their
footprints.

High doctrine about the text of hymns has been set out by John Wesley in a paragraph of his immortal Preface. I shall not deny myself the pleasure of quoting it:

'Many gentlemen have done my brother and me (though without naming us) the honour to reprint many of our hymns. Now they are perfectly welcome so to do, provided they print them just as they are. But I desire they would not attempt to mend them; for they really are not able. None of them is able to mend either the sense or the verse. Therefore, I must beg of them one of these two favours: either to let them stand just as they are, to take them for better for worse; or to add the true reading in the margin, or at the bottom of the page; that we may no longer be accountable either for the nonsense or for the doggerel of other men.'

Wesley's is high doctrine, and it is a pity that we cannot all attain to it; but we cannot. Barrett, you will notice, does almost all that Wesley asks. The advantage of some modification appears in one classical place: 'Rock of ages'. Toplady, I think, wrote 'While I draw this fleeting breath, When my eye-strings crack in death', and although we should not have complained, I imagine, if we had been brought up on that, it is difficult to believe that the now familiar 'When my eyes shall close in death' is not an improvement. Between this and Wesley's Preface the great mass of alterations falls. Besides this change in 'Rock of ages', Barrett could justify his version of 'When I survey the wondrous Cross' by his doctrine that the hymn is the composition 'as generally known'. 'On which the Prince of glory died' has so long displaced 'Where the young Prince of glory died' that the change cannot be called Barrett's. Yet we may doubt if it was á change originally worth making.

It is when we come to alterations—or, what is almost as bad, omissions because of 'offences against taste'—that we begin to breathe an electric atmosphere. The real objection to alterations in the interest of taste—taste of the 1880's or any time else—is this: alterations of that sort are all on the principle of the lowest common denominator; they resemble the process of attrition;

corners are rubbed off; peculiarities disappear; piquancy fails; one dead level is more and more approached. The good hymn as originally written could have been written by no one but its author. No one but Carlyle could write:

> With force of arms we nothing can,
>   Full soon were we down-ridden.
> But for us fights the Proper Man,
>   Whom God Himself hath bidden.

No one but Watts could write:

> What though we go the world around
>   And search from Britain to Japan,
> There shall be no religion found
>   So just to God, so safe for man.

No one but Charles Wesley could write:

> Adam, descended from above!
> Federal Head of all mankind,
>   The covenant of redeeming love
> In Thee let every sinner find.
>   Me, me, who still in darkness sit,
> Shut up in sin and unbelief,
>   Bring forth out of this hellish pit,
> This dungeon of despairing grief.

No one but a scholastic Doctor or a most able imitator of a scholastic Doctor could write:

> True God of true God,
> Light of Light Eternal, Lo He abhors not the Virgin's womb,
> Son of the Father, Begotten not created.

These are the words that contain and convey character; they make the hymn itself. They are peculiar, piquant, characteristic.

They are the enemies of taste. Taste omits, if it cannot prune them. Carlyle, says the man of taste, is too German, Watts too grotesque, Wesley too violent; the scholastic Doctor (or his imitator) too dogmatic. Let us have Mr. Symonds rather; not German nor grotesque nor violent nor dogmatic, not anything in fact.

> These things shall be! a loftier race
>   Than e'er the world hath known shall rise
> With flame of freedom in their souls
>   And light of knowledge in their eyes.
> They shall be gentle, brave and strong
>   To spill no drop of blood, but dare
> All that may plant man's lordship firm
>   On earth and fire and sea and air.

Or let us take refuge in Lord Houghton:

> Our lives enriched with gentle thoughts
>   And loving deeds may be,
> A stream that still the nobler grows
>   The nearer to the sea.

Nothing to offend taste there, because there is nothing that can be tasted. It is salt almost without savour; the L.C.D. of all good men; the religion of all sensible men; the very gospel of the men of goodwill.

This, then, being the pitfall of all who consider taste, let us see how well Dr. Barrett escaped it; and let us compare his performance with that of his successors. Barrett said no more than the truth when he said that he had been moderate in altering hymns in the cause of taste. Like Warren Hastings, he had cause to be astonished at his own moderation. He omitted a great many hymns, no doubt because he thought them in bad taste (many of Wesley's), but if he thought a hymn good, as a rule he let it stand unaltered. Taste, I am sure, made him omit that noble hymn on the Name of Jesus which should stand everywhere beside Newton's 'How sweet the name of Jesus sounds'. I mean

Jesus, the Name high over all
  In hell, or earth, or sky,
Angels and men before it fall,
  And devils fear and fly.

Jesus, the Name to sinners dear,
  The name to sinners given;
It scatters all their guilty fear,
  It turns their hell to heaven.

'Devils fearing and flying', I make no doubt, struck Dr. Barrett as bad taste. Even the mention of devils he seems generally to have disliked, and the state of taste in the 1880's certainly would not have allowed him to put baldly over a section of his book, as the Methodists had done, 'Describing Hell'. Before you smile, ponder this: Dr. Barrett's successors have carried his prejudices farther and, unless extremely pressed, consider the mention of angels and heaven in almost as bad taste as the mention of devils and hell. I must pause here to deplore our subservience to a fashion that has banished those splendidly truculent hymns which heartened our predecessors in hard times. As a change from our constant wail about the failure of the Church, I turn at times with satisfaction to the brave words of the men of old.

Into a world of ruffians sent
  I walk on hostile ground;
While human bears on slaughter bent
  And ravening wolves surround.

    .   .   .   .   .

Watch'd by the world's malignant eye,
  Who load us with reproach and shame,
As servants of the Lord Most high,
  As zealous for His glorious Name,
We ought in all His paths to move
With holy fear and humble love.

    .   .   .   .   .

Only have faith in God;
    In faith your foes assail;
Not wrestling against flesh and blood
    But all the powers of hell;
From thrones of glory driven,
    By flaming vengeance hurl'd,
They throng the air and darken heaven
    And rule the lower world.

On earth th' usurpers reign,
    Exert their baneful power;
O'er the poor fallen souls of men
    They tyrannize their hour.
But shall believers fear?
    But shall believers fly?
Or see the bloody cross appear
    And all their powers defy?

Jesu's tremendous name
    Puts all our foes to flight;
Jesus, the meek, the angry Lamb,
    A Lion is in fight.
By all hell's host withstood,
    We all hell's host o'erthrow,
And conquering them, through Jesu's blood,
    We still to conquer go.

One good example of the working of taste Dr. Barrett provided. He confesses that he altered Neale's version of Andrew of Crete's hymn 'Christian, dost thou see them'.

Christian! dost thou see them
    On the holy ground,
How the troops of Midian
    Prowl and prowl around?

So wrote Neale. Barrett found the reference to Midian, and (we may suspect) the word 'prowl', rather grotesque. 'The

troops of Midian' become the less unfamiliar 'powers of dark-
ness', who 'compass thee around' instead of prowling.

> How the powers of darkness
> Compass thee around.

A respectable couplet of which no one need be ashamed; but
it lacks the grip, I think, of the ruder original.

The alteration of the second verse illustrates a change due to
the doctrine, not taste. Neale wrote:

> Christian, dost thou feel them,
>   How they work within,
> Striving, tempting, luring,
>   Goading into sin?
> Christian, never tremble;
>   Never be down-cast;
> Smite them by the virtue
>   Of the Lenten fast.

Clearly this would never do; 'the virtue of the Lenten fast'
must be generalized for Dr. Barrett's constituency.

> Gird thee for the conflict;
>   Watch and pray and fast

does the trick. So used, the word 'fast' gives the rhyme and is
doctrinally innocuous.

With this compare the treatment by Dr. Barrett and by the
Methodists of Mrs. Alexander's hymn which was written for
St. Andrew's Day and is inspired by the narrative of his call:

> Jesus calls us; o'er the tumult
>   Of our life's wild, restless sea.
> Day by day His sweet voice soundeth,
>   Saying, 'Christian, follow me.'

> As of old St. Andrew heard it,
>   By the Galilean lake,
> Turned from home, and friends, and kindred,
>   Leaving all for His dear sake.

Whether Dr. Barrett thought that the mention of St. Andrew might lead to invocation of saints among modern Congregationalists, or that a hymn naming him could not be conveniently sung on any day but St. Andrew's Day, I do not know. For some reason he cut the verse out. He left the hymn perhaps better balanced without it, with its four verses now all built on one pattern, yet poorer (I think) by the loss of a personal allusion. The Methodists, ever diplomatic, have found a formula to appease all parties:

> As, of old, apostles heard it by the Galilean lake.

Dr. Barrett had warned people in advance that they would find in his book some hymns which were defective when tried by modern standards of taste, because they were closely connected with the experience of evangelical religion. He was as good as his word. He gave them unaltered what his successors have been too feeble to give, Cowper's noble and historic hymn, 'There is a fountain filled with blood, drawn from Immanuel's veins'. He did more. It might have been hard in 1883, though it was too easy in 1916, to suppress that well-loved hymn, but Barrett was under no definite obligation to add another hymn open to most of the objections that assail Cowper's, even to the use of the word 'veins'. Yet Barrett added Caswall's version of an Italian hymn:

> Glory be to Jesus,
>   Who, in bitter pains,
> Poured for me His Life-blood
>   From His sacred veins.
>
> Grace and life eternal
>   In that Blood I find;
> Blest be His compassion
>   Infinitely kind.

> Blest through endless ages
> Be the precious stream,
> Which from endless torments
> Doth the world redeem.

This proves Barrett's courage. He went against the taste of his time and added to the rock of offence because he knew that this hymn, charged with a simple childlike piety, was too good to be unknown among Congregationalists.

Why, then, if we grant his courage—as we must—why did he suppress that verse of 'When I survey the wondrous Cross' which has now almost passed from memory?

> His dying crimson like a robe
> Spreads o'er His body on the tree;
> Then am I dead to all the globe;
> And all the globe is dead to me.

It is strange and inexcusable, the worst blot on Barrett's fame.

In Barrett, then, in 1883 we can see the beginnings of that painful bowdlerization of hymns that still continues. Barrett is struggling with the tendency new in his times, now giving way unexpectedly, now carrying reprisals into the enemy's camp. His successors have not usually altered this sort of expression: they simply drop the hymn. Even the Methodists, we note in passing, are guilty. They had enriched hymnology beyond all others by hymns on the death of Christ, but their glory is become their shame. I do not speak of hymns which were perhaps needlessly and unscripturally trying to modern taste:

> My Jesus to know and to feel His Blood flow,
> 'Tis life everlasting, 'tis heaven below.

I speak of the fanatical prejudice against solemn words.

O Thou eternal Victim, slain
A sacrifice for guilty man,
By the eternal Spirit made
An offering in the sinner's stead;
Our everlasting Priest art Thou
And plead'st Thy death for sinners now.

Thy offering still continues new;
Thy vesture keeps its bloody hue;
Thou stand'st the ever-slaughtered Lamb;
Thy priesthood still remains the same;
Thy years, O God, can never fail;
Thy goodness is unchangeable.

That, one of the greatest Communion hymns written by Wesley, cannot be made other than it is: a hymn about life by death and healing by blood. If the idea is repugnant to modern taste, there is a case for allowing modern taste to starve itself still further by banishing the hymn entirely. There is no case for doing what the modern Methodists do: they rewrite one line. 'Thy vesture keeps its bloody hue' becomes 'Thy vesture keeps its crimson hue'. You cannot tinker with the stupendous things: you must take them or leave them. If the catholic and Evangelical doctrine of atonement by the blood of Christ be true, no expression of it can be too strong; all, on the contrary, must be too weak. And if it is not true, you want not dilution of it, but abandonment. This is what our modern editors will not see.

Their blindness does not depart when they pass from the Atonement. An example, peculiarly flagrant, occurs in the *Congregational Hymnary* among the Pentecost hymns. For this festival, Keble wrote his classical 'When God of old came down from heaven'. Not even our modernists could ignore this; they had, anyhow, a feeling for Pentecost as one of the vaguer feasts. Nor could they claim that the hymn was too long to be printed— at least as Barrett had printed it; they had themselves printed far worse hymns at infinitely greater length. And yet—and yet, they could not keep their bungling hands off Keble. That second verse:

> Around the trembling mountain's base
>   The prostrate people lay,
> A day of wrath and not of grace,
>   A dim and dreadful day.

It gave a horrid notion of God; that was indeed very unpleasant. To be sure, it is exactly what the Bible says happened at Sinai, and, after all, it is about Sinai that Keble writes. But it is not the modernist's notion of God; and since by his nature he cannot be honest and say, 'Scrap Sinai; scrap Moses; scrap this O.T. revelation; it is not true', he says, 'I will keep just enough of Keble to flatter myself that there is no break with the tradition (that is bad form—like the old Dissenters), but not enough to convey any particular meaning. Keble's aim, it is true, was to contrast Sinai and Pentecost and yet to connect them. I will keep both, cutting out both contrast and connexion. I will so make the best (or worst) of both worlds'. Encouraged, he proceeds and reads next:

> The fires, that rush'd on Sinai down
>   In sudden torrents dread,
> Now gently light, a glorious crown,
>   On every sainted head.

> And as on Israel's awe-struck ear
>   The voice exceeding loud,
> The trump, that angels quake to hear,
>   Thrilled from the deep, dark cloud;

> So, when the Spirit of our God
>   Came down His flock to find,
> A voice from Heav'n was heard abroad,
>   A rushing, mighty wind.

Here we have two signs of Pentecost, the fire and wind, with their types at Sinai. The editors of the *Hymnary* leave us the wind, but cut out the flames of fire. To the plain man they stand or fall together. Either something unusual happened at Pentecost or nothing unusual happened. If nothing—well, why waste a breezy Whitsunday morning by singing about it at all? You had better be at golf. If something worth singing about happened, why strain out the flame and swallow the wind, as the editors of the *Hymnary* do? Well, for this reason. If you are ingenious you can believe that that first Whitsunday was a very windy day and that the early Christians, not being ingenious, but simple, thought the wind had some connexion with a spiritual experience which they agreed to call the Holy Ghost. You can retain the verse about the wind and so preserve the tradition of Keble's verses and your self-respecting intellect. But the verse about the flame is more difficult. To retain it commits one (if pressed) to more than a windy day at Pentecost. A thunderstorm with lightning seems the obvious way out, but to ask for a combination of both wind and fire on the same day as the Christians had their experience of the Holy Ghost is asking perhaps a little too much of historical coincidence, generous though that goddess of the critic may be. It reduces the risks to cut out the flame; and, anyhow, tradition and our face are saved without it. I do not suggest that this form of argument was openly followed on the editorial board which produced the *Hymnary:* but, though unexpressed, that state of mind underlay the choice of certain verses and the omission of others. And it is of all states of mind in which hymns can be selected and altered the most dangerous, dishonest, and damnable. It is ludicrous, too; but that is nothing.

This same unwillingness to face certain simple facts and make up one's mind one way or the other about them has in the last forty years wrought another set of weakening changes in what were sturdy hymns. Barrett sometimes shrank from calling a spade a spade; but his successors shrink more often. If you open a book like *Worship Song*, you detect the faint odour of a literary

Keating's Powder: a sort of spiritual insect killer—fatal to
worms. The elder hymn-writers delighted in worms. Doddridge even wrote of our Lord that

> Sinful worms to Him are given,
> A colony to people heaven.

The elder hymn-writers overdid it. We weary of the metaphor, exact and scriptural as it is. But our delicate-souled editors
pursue the worm with a cruelty and diligence altogether beyond
its deserts. You would suppose, would you not? that among
decent men the writer of such princely stuff as this might be
allowed one metaphor of his own choosing:

> Angels and men, resign your claim
> To pity, mercy, love, and grace;
> These glories crown Jehovah's name
> With an incomparable blaze.
> Who is a pardoning God like Thee
> Or who has grace so rich and free?

But he also wrote:

> Crimes of such horror to forgive,
> Such guilty daring worms to spare.

Where is the Keating's Powder? The Congregational Union's
Committee did not fail to extirpate the worms.

> Such dire offences to forgive,
> Such guilty daring *souls* to spare.

That is less offensive in several ways. 'Dire offences', if you
come to think of it, is quite a non-committal phrase. 'Dire'—
no one in ordinary life uses that word, so no one minds it being
attached to his 'offences'. Yet the people to whom much is
forgiven love much. It was the forgiveness of 'crimes of such

horror' (not of these 'dire offences') that provoked the ecstatic cry:

> In wonder lost, with trembling joy
>   We take our pardon from our God,
> Pardon for crimes of deepest dye,
>   A pardon bought with Jesu's blood.

No one is going to be lost in wonder about 'dire offences': make no mistake about that. It is the same pettifogging spirit that is at work in Prayer Book revision. The modern Anglican does not wish to call himself a miserable sinner, a miserable offender, to say that the burden of his sins is intolerable. He is not a miserable sinner, but an honest seeker after truth: the burden of his sins is not intolerable, imperceptible rather. Very well, but don't expect to be able to pass on to what the Methodists used to call 'The Pleasantness and Excellence of Religion' unless you have known the section 'For Mourners convinced of Sin'. Our editors are in the same state of mind as Mr. Chesterton's mob which shouted not 'No Popery', but 'Not quite so much Popery'. Well, the Pope cares little for such mobs; and Satan, who

> Trembles when he sees
> The weakest saint upon his knees,

trembles little before congregations that are too discreet to call themselves saints and too genteel to call themselves sinners.

One example of a change for doctrinal reasons, and I end this part of my paper. Doddridge, as good a Dissenter as most of us need wish to be, wrote a Communion hymn. He wrote it in the eighteenth century. He wrote it, that is to say, before people had begun to suppose that the only proper doctrine for Dissenters is the so-called Zwinglian doctrine, the doctrine that the Lord's Supper is a memorial feast and nothing more. He wrote, therefore:

> Hail sacred feast which Jesus makes,
> Rich banquet of His flesh and blood.
> Thrice happy he who here partakes
> That sacred stream, that heavenly food.

Barrett, since he printed Keble's communion hymn,

> Fresh from the atoning sacrifice
> The world's Redeemer bleeding lies,
> That man His foe for whom He bled
> May take Him as his daily bread,

could hardly complain of Doddridge's; and he let it stand. But it offends some; and you will find elsewhere the meaning weakened and watered down:

> Rich banquet of His flesh and blood.

Even that is too much and it becomes:

> Sweet emblems of His flesh and blood.

Poor Doddridge is suspected of Popery by our lovers of the feeble. One change in this hymn Barrett did make lower down.

> Why are these dainties still in vain
> Before unwilling hearts displayed?

wrote the unblushing Doddridge. But 'dainties', we must agree, is too much; especially if your memory of the Methodist hymn reinforces the objection:

> O bid the wretched sons of need
> On soul-reviving dainties feed.

For 'dainties' read 'emblems', says Barrett. Since 'emblems' is distinctly out of harmony with the thought of the hymn it would probably be better simply to respect Doddridge's own word, 'banquet'—'Why is the banquet still in vain?'

This same hymn introduces what I want to say about the place we Dissenters give to hymns in divine service. You remember that the hymn contains an interesting, startling word:

> Was not for you the victim slain?
> Are you forbid the children's bread?

'Victim': that is hardly the expression that conventional notions lead us to expect a Protestant Dissenter, writing in the basest of Latitudinarian times, to use at the Lord's Table? 'Victim': it is the word of the Roman Mass, too strong for the Book of Common Prayer. It is the highest of high sacrificial doctrine. Yes, but it is *there*. Doddridge said it.

Now hear Wesley. There is between the Wolds and the sea in Wesley's county (and mine) within tolerable distance of Lincoln Cathedral, the pitiful ruin of Bardney Abbey, left as Henry VIII and his followers left it, when they had no more use for it. They had melted down the bells and the lead on the roof and had stolen the sacred vessels. You may see the place in the centre of the nave of the abbey church where they lit their fire and melted the lead; and you may see more. You may see close by, unharmed because it was only of use to pious men, the altar of the five wounds of Christ, with its five signs of the Cross; one in each corner and one in the centre. Who thought of this or the five wounds in eighteenth-century England? Who preserved the continuity of Christian devotion in Bardney? Not those Anglican farmers of Bardney who carted away the abbey stones to build their cowsheds. But Wesley was teaching their Methodist labourers that same catholic and evangelical faith, that 'Enthusiasm', hateful to bishops and scorned by modernists, in almost the same accents as the Bardney monks had known. Within a stone's-throw of the altar of the five wounds, the Methodists were singing:

> Weary souls, that wander wide
>   From the central point of bliss,
> Turn to Jesus crucified,
>   Fly to those dear wounds of His.
>
> .   .   .   .   .
>
> Five bleeding wounds He bears,
>   Received on Calvary;
> They pour effectual prayers,
>   They strongly plead for me.

It is odd, is it not? to find the language of medieval devotion coming back on the lips, not of archbishops and deans in apostolic succession, but of Doddridge and Wesley. This language, these images of

> The Master's marred and wounded mien,
> His hands, His feet, His side

(to use Montgomery's words), I am aware, have come once again to be familiar in the thoughts and speech of all English Christians, Anglican and Nonconformist. They could not indeed be lost permanently unless Christian emotion was itself to perish. They had been wrongfully suppressed by the Arianism and Latitudinarianism of the eighteenth century. But the way of their return: that it is that interests me, first by hymns and afterwards by catholic ornaments. It reminds us of the possibility (or is it a probability?) that the modern Romish worship of the Sacred Heart of Jesus owes something to a devotional book by Oliver Cromwell's Congregational chaplain, Thomas Goodwin, *The Heart of Christ in Heaven towards Sinners on Earth.*

So, in piety, do extremes agree: Catholic and Evangelical meet, and kiss one another at the Cross.

Hymns are for us Dissenters what the liturgy is for the Anglican. They are the framework, the setting, the conventional, the traditional part of divine service as we use it. They are, to adopt the language of the liturgiologists, the Dissenting Use. That is why we understand and love them as no one else does. You have only to attend Anglican services to discover that the Anglican, though he can write a hymn, cannot use it. It does not fit the Prayer Book service. The Anglican, because he has what Borrow justly called 'England's sublime liturgy', has been careless of other liturgies, like the liturgy of hymns. He has about as much feeling for the correct liturgical use of hymns as Dr. Orchard has for the correct liturgical use of collects; I cannot put it stronger or fairer. It is with hymns and collects as (they say) it is with 'hands' in riding—you must be born with them. An Anglican clergyman to whom in other respects no one could deny the adjective 'educated' will choose as a hymn before a sermon:

> O worship the King
> All glorious above.

This is a tolerable rhyme, useful to usher in late-comers, but a most inadequate preparation for the Preaching of the Word. What that august occasion demands a Methodist local preacher knows by instinct:

> Come, Holy Ghost, for moved by Thee
>   The Prophets wrote and spoke.
> Unlock the Truth, Thyself the key,
>   Unseal the sacred Book.

Or:

> Inspirer of the Ancient Seers
>   Who wrote from Thee the sacred page,
> The same through all succeeding years
>   To us in our degenerate age,
> The Spirit of Thy word impart
> And breathe the life into our heart.

And what is true of Anglicans is almost as true of Presbyterians. They have their metrical psalms. They can use them; we cannot. Nor do we understand the use of paraphrases as the

Presbyterians do. How terrible a loss this is a very little experience of Presbyterian worship will soon teach us. On the other
hand, we English Free Churchmen have little to learn from
Anglicans or from Scotland about the use of hymns. We mark
times and seasons, celebrate festivals, express experiences, and
expound doctrines by hymns.[1] There is, I believe, but one
hymn with which the Wesleyan Conference can open its
annual session, 'For the Society on meeting':

> And are we yet alive
>> And see each other's face?
> Glory and praise to Jesus give
>> For His redeeming grace.
>
> What troubles have we seen,
>> What conflicts have we past,
> Fightings without and fears within
>> Since we assembled last.

There is one hymn without which no Watch-Night service
is complete:

> Come, let us anew
> Our journey pursue,
> Roll round with the year,
> And never stand still till the Master appear.

[1] The two village services which I attended on Easter Day perfectly illustrate this
contrast between the Anglicans and ourselves. In the Parish Church there was
appropriate liturgical celebration of the Resurrection: the Proper Preface in the Communion, the Easter Collect, and in place of the *Venite* commonly sung at Matins the
special Anthem, 'Christ our Passover is sacrificed for us, therefore let us keep the
feast'. Those things any person familiar with the Prayer Book could prophesy would
come; but the hymns were a gamble. One could not be sure what the Vicar would
choose. I feared the worst and I was right. But in the evening at the chapel, though
I was uncertain about the prayers, there was no gamble about the hymns. I *knew* we
should have Charles Wesley's Easter hymn, 'Christ the Lord is risen to-day', with its
twenty-four 'Alleluias'; and we did have it. Among any Dissenters worth the name
that hymn is as certain to come on Easter Day as the Easter Collect in the Established Church. And mark this further—those twenty-four 'Alleluias' are not there
for nothing: the special use of 'Alleluia' at Easter comes down to us from the most
venerable liturgies. Our hymns are our liturgy, an excellent liturgy. Let us study it,
respect it, use it, develop it, and boast of it.

We recite no Creed, because our hymns are full of the form of sound words:

> Let earth and heaven combine,
>   Angels and men agree,
> To praise in songs Divine
>   The Incarnate Deity,
> Our God contracted to a span,
> Incomprehensibly made man.

'The Father incomprehensible, the Son incomprehensible, the Holy Ghost incomprehensible': it is the word of the Athanasian Creed. Every clause in the Nicene and in the Athanasian Creed has its parallel in our hymn-books; and if we use no crucifix, no stations of the Cross, no processions, no banners, no incense, you must attribute it not to the fancy that we have neither need nor understanding of what these things represent. We do not use these things because our hymns revive the sacred scenes and stir the holy emotions with a power and a purity denied to all but the greatest craftsmen. There *are* pictures of the Crucifixion that rival, and perhaps excel, the passion hymns of Watts and Wesley; but those pictures are to be sought in distant lands by the few and the wealthy for a few moments only. The hymn-book offers masterpieces for all who have an ear to hear, every day and in every place, to every worshipper. When I am informed that Dissenting worship is bare and cold, making no appeal to the emotions because it does not employ the tawdry and flashy productions of fifth-rate ecclesiastical art-mongers, I am at no loss for an answer. I am only at a loss when I am asked to explain why, holding these treasures, we turn so often from them—the great passionate, doctrinal, emotional hymns—to the pedestrian rhymers of ethical commonplaces.

Out of all this come two sets of general observations. If you grant that this is, at least among us Dissenters, the true place of the hymn in worship, it follows, first, that the selection of the hymns, the setting of the framework upon which the whole service is to hang, the choice of the liturgy for the day, this goes, of right and of duty, to the minister. The selection of hymns by organists and choirmasters, or the gambling of them between the organist and the minister in the vestry ten minutes before the service begins—these are abuses that explain the confusion of thought that marks the progress of our services. You cannot tell where you will be next, what has been done, what is still to come. The separate parts of the service are not distinct, not articulated. There are two prayers. But what is the difference except the difference of length? It is often hard to tell. The same ground is traversed in each; too hurriedly first and afterwards at too leisurely a pace. And the hymns, if chosen at random, traverse the same ground. I take an extreme example: if a minister chooses (as he never should) that general jail-delivery hymn of Bonar, 'When the weary, seeking rest, to Thy goodness flee', he has clearly provided for general intercessions at that service with more than ample adequacy. He ought not to do it all over again in his prayer, and (if he thinks of what he is doing) he will not. But if Bonar's hymn is let off at him at the last minute by an organist who likes the tune (and such there be) and if the minister has provided for intercession on the same lines in his prayer, then either he must improvise a fresh plan of service and prayer or he must repeat the same feature of service— two very bad things. Don't tell me that I have forgotten the tune problem. I have not. I allow the organist all his rights there; and I will not bar him from the absolute choice of some few hymns, if he selects them well in advance, and informs the minister before the minister plans his service. But as I protected the text of the hymns from the antiquarian, so I would protect their tunes from the mere musician. The glory of God, not of composers or even of organ-builders, is the end of divine service.

My second observation turns on this question, which, having suffered so much, you have a right to put to me: What do you think makes a good hymn? And, as some would go on, Why cannot we write good hymns to-day? In answer to the second part of that question I should reply that we both can and do write good hymns to-day. They are, no doubt, difficult to discover; but at all times people have found it difficult to discover good things in their contemporaries. Good things have always been easily smothered by rubbish, as they are to-day; and you must give the rubbish time to die down. The nineteenth century, as I have tried to show, produced some great hymns, some of the greatest; but it is not until the Havergals and the Fabers begin to droop and wither that we can see what is truly good. I make no question but that it is the same to-day. 'Wait and see' is the only wise, as it is the only liberal, policy.

We return to the other part of the inquiry: What makes a good hymn? Two groups of hymns—the evangelical hymns of the eighteenth century and the medieval hymns of the Latin Church—may supply the answer. These seem to me to be our best hymns. No competent critic, I think, will deny that they are very good. Now, if you look at the evangelical group, you notice two things. First, these hymns combine personal experience with a presentation of historic events and doctrines. Full of the intensest and most individual passion as they are, they contain more than that: the writers look back from their own experience to those experiences of the Incarnate Son of God on which their faith was built. This gives them a steadiness, a firmness, a security against mere emotionalism and sentimentality which more recent writers, trying to lay bare their souls, have found it difficult to avoid. Look first, for instance, at this nineteenth-century hymn:

> I lift my heart to Thee,
>   Saviour Divine;
> For Thou art all to me,
>   And I am Thine.
> Is there on earth a closer bond than this,
> That 'My Beloved's mine and I am His'?

> To Thee, Thou bleeding Lamb,
>   I all things owe;
> All that I have and am,
>   And all I know.
> All that I have is now no longer mine,
> And I am not mine own; Lord, I am Thine.

I choose purposely a hymn of unquestionable sincerity and of doctrine as like as may be to that of the eighteenth-century evangelical so that no extraneous differences may confuse the issue. But, though the hymn is not without merit, you notice the almost morbid self-consciousness of the writer. Throughout five verses he ploughs through his own hopes and experiences and emotions and has hardly time to make even an indirect reference to anything outside his own feelings.[1]

A great hymn of the eighteenth century describing a similar frame of mind and heart is familiar enough to us all. Notice how rapidly it glances from the writer's experience to the divine experience and passion that is the very foundation of the writer's hope:

> And can it be, that I should gain
>   An interest in the Saviour's blood?
> Died He for me who caused His pain?
>   For me who Him to death pursued?
> Amazing love! how can it be
> That Thou, my God, should'st die for me?

> He left His Father's throne above,
>   So free, so infinite His grace,
> Emptied Himself of all but love
>   And bled for Adam's helpless race;
> 'Tis mercy all, immense and free;
> For O my God it found out me.

[1] The same is almost true of 'O Love, that will not let me go'.

> Long my imprison'd spirit lay
>   Fast bound in sin and nature's night;
> Thine eye diffused a quick'ning ray;
>   I woke; the dungeon flam'd with light;
> My chains fell off; my heart was free,
> I rose, went forth, and followed Thee.

It is not less personal than the other hymn but it is less introspective and has more of a godward quality. And notice how carefully the writer expresses his experience of liberation in the words of St. Peter's deliverance from prison. It is as if, knowing how difficult it is to express religious emotion without nauseating sentimentality, he were timid about going outside the language already well tested for the expression of religious emotion, individual as his emotion may be.[1]

You have the supreme example of this transmuting our own experience into a classical, scriptural, authorized form, purging out all unworthy self-centredness and yet keeping expression all the more alive for the change, in the greatest of Charles Wesley's hymns, 'Come, O Thou Traveller unknown'. Here, under the form of Jacob wrestling with the angel, Wesley tells of his own spiritual conversion.

It is this quality, I am persuaded, that John Wesley had in mind when he commended his brother's hymns as *Scriptural*. It was a merit in Wesley's eyes, not because of any rigidly bibliolatrous notions, but partly because, as a scholar and a gentleman, he liked to see great things clothed in great language.

And this brings us to the other quality of these eighteenth-century hymn-writers. They were trained in the school of the Greek and Latin classics. This gave them, not only a knowledge of metre and a facility in verse-making that no other training can give, but also a mastery of the art of allusion—deft, relevant, and appropriate. What he had done at Westminster and Oxford to the mythology, the poets, and the orators of Greece and Rome, Charles Wesley in later life continued to do to the Scriptures.

[1] Contrast in the same way consecutive hymns in the *Hymnal*, the nineteenth-century Bubier's 'I would commune with Thee, my God' with Wesley's 'Talk with us, Lord, Thyself reveal'.

That is one of the reasons why almost every verse of his 2,000 hymns contains a scriptural allusion.

You see what this meant, not only for Charles Wesley, but for all that antiquity-ridden century. It had, because of the form of its secular education, a training in expressing its own experience in conventional images which few recent writers have had. The age of the romantic poets that followed produced greater poetry, but lesser hymns. Hymn-writers follow, at a distance, the fashions of writing prevalent in the highest circles; and as long as poetic thought of all sorts found a strictly metrical expression, the hymn-writers (who *must* use rather rigid metres) could work easily because they were swimming with the current of their day. After the romantic poets had burst the bonds of metre and no self-respecting person wrote 'verses' any more, the hymn-writer found himself fighting against the current of poetic fashion or left in a backwater. The best people no longer wrote L.M. or S.M. or C.M. or 6·8s, but only P.M. (peculiar metre). The classical art of allusion to well-known events and the use of conventional metaphors were now taken to be the sign of an inferior mind; and if there be anything in my contention about the value of a union of personal experience with references to the historic events on which the Faith is built, it is clear that the nineteenth-century hymn-writers were at a disadvantage. They tried to express themselves in language mostly their own. They borrowed less from the rich treasury of the Christian classics—the Scriptures.

The other class of the greatest hymns that I mentioned—the medieval Latin and Greek hymns—illustrates a similar thesis. What is the almost magical charm of hymns like 'All glory, laud, and honour' and 'O happy band of pilgrims'? No one can say with certainty, but simplicity—simplicity of thought and of expression, the simplicity of children and the Kingdom of Heaven—is an element in it. And the simplicity, if you look closely at it, consists in this: the writer takes an event in the life of our Lord and after the plainest mention of it joins with it some petition or reflexion which concerns his own life.

> The people of the Hebrews
>   With palms before Thee went;
> Our praise and prayer and anthems
>   Before Thee we present.
> To Thee before Thy Passion
>   They sang their hymns of praise;
> To Thee now high exalted
>   Our melody we raise.
>
> The Cross that Jesus carried
>   He carried as your due;
> The Crown that Jesus weareth
>   He weareth it for you.

It is the art that conceals art; but I believe the elements are the same as in the great eighteenth-century hymns.

And, lastly, the greatest hymns are Christian, thoroughly and irrevocably Christian; and when I say Christian I mean that they concern Christ, not that they are what is called Christian in spirit, or indirectly or unconsciously Christian:

> My heart is full of Christ, and longs
>   Its glorious matter to declare.
> Of Him I make my loftier songs . . .

That is the confession of the greatest hymn-writers. They go back to the New Testament, and especially to the Gospels. They are not merely theistic, like the psalm paraphrases: great as some of those are, they miss the highest note. Even 'O God of Bethel' or 'Through all the changing scenes of life' strikes with a faint chill of Old Testament theology the disciple who has sat at the feet of Jesus. Still less are the greatest hymn-songs of human aspiration or of human fellowship. Dare I say it? Bunyan's pilgrim song is not among the greatest hymns for precisely this reason. I know its excellencies; I yield to no one in love of Bunyan; but there, at any rate, he does not go deep enough. Not good fellowship, but Christ, is the subject of the greatest hymns.

That is why all the greatest hymns are orthodox, and why we Dissenters have preserved intact (even better than Churches with more elaborate safeguards) the full catholic and evangelical faith. Hymns are the safest protection and the surest vehicle of orthodoxy. The language of the sublimest hymns in all ages and in all communions is the same:

> Thou art the King of Glory, O Christ;
> Thou art the everlasting Son of the Father.
> When Thou tookest upon Thee to deliver man
> Thou didst not abhor the Virgin's womb.
> When Thou hadst overcome the sharpness of death
> Thou didst open the Kingdom of Heaven to all believers.

So says the *Te Deum* and Charles Wesley goes on:

> Then let us sit beneath His cross
>   And gladly catch the healing stream:
> All things for Him account but loss
>   And give up all our hearts to Him.
> Of nothing think or speak beside,
> My Lord, my Love, is crucified.